Penguin Nature Guides

Birds

of Wood, Park and Garden

Lars Jonsson

Translated from the Swedish by Roger Tanner
Edited by Jim Flegg

Penguin Books

Penguin Books Ltd, Harmondsworth,
Middlesex, England
Penguin Books, 625 Madison Avenue,
New York, New York 10022, U.S.A.
Penguin Books Australia Ltd, Ringwood,
Victoria, Australia
Penguin Books Canada Ltd, 2801 John Street,
Markham, Ontario, Canada L3R 1B4
Penguin Books (N.Z.) Ltd, 182–190 Wairau Road,
Auckland 10, New Zealand

Fåglar i naturen: Skog, park, trädgård
first published by Wahlström & Widstrand 1977
This translation published 1978

Text and illustrations copyright © Lars Jonsson, 1976
Copyright © in the English edition: Penguin Books Ltd, 1978
All rights reserved

Printed in Portugal by Gris Impressores, Cacém
Filmset in Monophoto Times by
Northumberland Press Ltd, Gateshead, Tyne and Wear

Contents

Preface

From my study window and elsewhere, I have had innumerable opportunities during the past few years of studying house sparrows and tree sparrows, two of the commonest suburban residents. One winter about four years ago, I decided to try to obtain some form of 'definitive' knowledge of the colour, markings, shape and movements of the house sparrow – to specify its general appearance. These birds gather outside my window at almost any time of day, and I usually have a sketching pad on my desk so that I can draw new sketches at a second's notice. To my astonishment, however, I constantly discover new lines and shapes, new colours and patterns, new traits of behaviour, new postures, and the upshot is that I am unable to produce a definitive picture even of such a well-known species as the house sparrow! Understandably, then, I feel dwarfed by the task of depicting and describing the birds of a whole continent.

Within the limited amount of printed space I have tried to bring out what is not already apparent from the illustrations, and I hope that the reader will be able to translate the pictorial descriptions into words. I should add that, while perfectly aware of the disadvantages of a non-systematic presentation, I believe that these disadvantages are offset by the benefits of dividing the birds into habitat groupings.

I wish to extend a special word of acknowledgement to Stellan Hedgren for close and indispensable cooperation. I would also like to thank the many friends who have generously encouraged me with their views on the design and content of this book, particularly Gunnar Brusewitz, Håkan Delin, Lars Fält, Stig Holmstedt, Wolf Jenning and Lars Svensson.

L. J.

Introduction

This is the first of five books which cover all bird species regularly nesting or occurring in Europe. It deals with those birds which inhabit all types of forest or woodland, parkland and gardens in Europe south of the northern coniferous forests and north of the Mediterranean countries and the Alps. The term 'forest or woodland' used here includes continuous areas of deciduous, coniferous and mixed woodland together with residues of woodland in the cultivated landscape such as spinneys, copses and scrub.

In classifying species in this way, according to environment or habitat, the problem arises of where to put those birds which occur in several types of natural surroundings. This applies particularly to birds found both in forest or woodland and in farmland, as the cultivated landscape has gradually evolved through the felling and cultivation of forests and the draining of bogs and swamps. This makes it natural for the birdlife of the cultivated landscape and of forest and woodland to overlap.

Bird species vary a great deal in the degree of the attachment to woodland in its various forms (see p. 7). Some depend on forest and woodland throughout the year for food and breeding, while others find food from open fields and meadows and only nest in the forest itself. In deciding where to put those species for which more than one location was possible, we have considered the practicalities of field recognition. Thus species like the hobby, whinchat, stonechat, yellowhammer, the ortolan and cirl bunting, all partly found in thinly wooded country, gardens and scrub, have been excluded from this book. The same goes for such species as the heron, osprey and green sandpiper which breed in wooded country but are really water birds. There are also a number of species which may be occasional visitors to the area with which we are concerned. Northern and eastern species (nutcracker, waxwing, Siberian tit, pine grosbeak, the crossbill species and others) may in certain years be found to some extent outside their true distribution area. Rare, stray specimens from Asia, southern Europe and America are also liable to appear. From the edge of the wood and overhead the birdwatcher can look out over a lake or seashore and see many other species. But the attachment of bird species to their particular environments is still a natural and prominent characteristic.

Birds in their environment

If one morning towards the end of May you sit down on a wooded slope, you may think you are surrounded by an odd assortment of birdlife. Tree tops, bushes and the ground will be full of singing birds – willow warblers, chaffinches, wrens, robins and woodpigeons. Before long you will note a certain regularity in the ways the different birds behave. A willow warbler darts along the thin branches of a sallow bush, snapping up barely visible insects from among the small leaves – but a wood warbler, although almost identical, seems to prefer the high branches of a beech tree. A great tit, pestered by its young – which have already learned to fly – is combing broad-leaved bushes and thickets, picking butterfly larvae from the leaves – while a coal tit, although quite similar to its relative, prefers conifer branches. The pied flycatcher shoos away fellow members of the species from near the tree where it is nesting, yet four pairs of starlings nest quietly in a single tree.

This is how to discover that most species specialize in a particular kind of food in a particular part of forest or wood, or even part of a tree, and that they nest in special holes or forks in a particular type of natural surrounding or habitat. They make more or less rigid demands of their surroundings or have adapted to the different environments in forest or wood. The parts of a forest or wood differ from each other in their supply of food, cavities and tree forks for nesting, song perches and shelter from enemies. In the course of evolution, species have developed that can subsist on the conditions applying in quite closely defined areas. Warblers have the physiology for catching small insects from tree branches, bushes and shrubs. Woodpeckers can live on insects from inside tree trunks and birds of prey have bills and feet for catching other birds and small mammals. Birds vary a great deal, however, in the extent to which they specialize in a particular environment and a particular item of food. Crows, being omnivores, are found in many types of landscape, while crossbills inhabit only coniferous forests. As long as the environment remains unaltered, its conditions regulate the type of species and their numbers. This is a complex and delicate web of life in which all constituent parts are interdependent. In many cases it is not exactly clear which factors influence the combination and numbers of species and to what extent. Of the factors known to us, three seem to be of primary importance: the occurrence of food, nesting places and predators.

Food

Changes affect highly specialized species more than those which adjust easily to new surroundings. The lesser spotted woodpecker, which lives on insects in decayed or decaying tree branches, is seriously affected by the removal of diseased and fallen trees. The great spotted woodpecker, on the other hand, has a broader diet of tree insects, pine cone seeds, fruit, eggs and nestlings and is less sensitive to such changes. An increase in food supplies leads to population growth (if no other limiting factors intervene). One striking example is the increase in siskins and crossbills in years when spruce trees have produced plenty of seed and there is an abundant supply of cones.

The food supply can be a regulating factor. Owls, often dependent on small rodents, match their reproduction rate to the supply. In years when few rodents are available they can 'refrain' from breeding altogether, while in good years they can lay 10 eggs instead of the normal four, five or six. Food shortage has a more direct influence by causing a large percentage of the population to die of starvation.

There is a connexion between temperature and food: the colder the weather, the more energy birds require. Wrens, which are sedentary in Britain during winter, die in large numbers during really cold winters. The food supply becomes too meagre for them to be able, during the short days, to accumulate a large enough energy reserve to maintain their body temperature overnight.

The presence of a species in a particular area during the year also depends on the food supply available. Birds living exclusively on insects migrate south in winter, while seed eaters have a better chance of remaining more stationary, because there are seeds on trees, herbaceous plants and the ground even in winter. Seasonal changes also bring local fluctuations in supply, thus affecting numbers. Jays, nutcrackers and nuthatches in search of nuts may invade a hazel coppice during late summer and autumn and yet be rarely seen there at other times. A good local supply of beechmast often attracts hordes of tits and finches during autumn and winter, but during the rest of the year many of these birds reside elsewhere. The blue tit nests in deciduous and mixed woodland, but during autumn and winter it often ventures into reed-beds for larvae and chrysalids. The great tit, on the other hand, usually eats only vegetable food in winter and is therefore a more permanent resident of deciduous and mixed woodland than the blue tit.

Nesting places

All birds, to a greater or lesser extent, are particular about where they breed, making availability of suitable nesting places, song perches and sheltering vegetation a regulating factor. The distribution of cavity-nesting species such as the pied flycatcher and stock dove depends upon their finding suitable cavities. This search is one reason why many species nest in human settlements.

Predators

Predators are another primary regulating factor. Birds of prey, crows, foxes, squirrels, badgers, weasels, rats and snakes take a heavy toll of eggs, nestlings and adult birds. The importance of predation as a reducing factor varies considerably from one place or species to another. It is not uncommon for 60 or 70 per cent of the woodpigeon's eggs to be taken by predators, while only a small percentage of the sparrowhawk's eggs, for instance, are taken.

The different environments of forest and woodland

The continuing changes wrought, mostly by man, in forest and woodland (and in the natural environment as a whole) influence the factors determining the type of birdlife that occurs. The modern environmental changes which have almost completely destroyed or transformed most of the ancient forests of Europe have also radically transformed the structure of the bird population. The primitive forest, untouched by man, was usually a mixture of deciduous trees, conifers and bushes. The trees died natural deaths and lay where they fell, new ones gradually sprang up, and in this way a whole variety of environmental conditions developed. In a forest of this kind there is a distinct vertical zonation into a ground layer (mosses, lichens and fungi), field layer (herbs, grasses, small bushes, tree seedlings), a bush layer (woody herbaceous plants, bushes, saplings) and a tree layer. This stratification also implies maximum utilization of light. Untouched mixed forests, where all strata are well developed, have the greatest diversity of plant species and therefore the widest variety of seeds and insects, which in turn sustain an abundance of birdlife. Monocultures, such as spruce, pine and beech plantations, are usually dark, with relatively small numbers of plants beneath them in their field and bush layers, thus excluding those species which depend on these layers for their food.

Many species, however, adjust to new surroundings if food is available. The sparrowhawk, tawny owl, woodpigeon, jackdaw, blackbird, song thrush and robin are all instances of sylvan species which have adjusted to

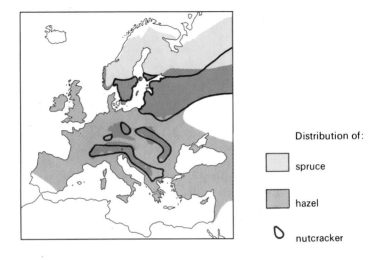

Distribution of:

☐ spruce

▨ hazel

◖ nutcracker

Often a combination of conditions must exist for a species to survive and reproduce in an area. The nutcracker, which prefers to nest in dense spruce forests, is not found north of a certain boundary in Europe, even though there are many such forests in Scandinavia, for instance. Instead, its northern boundary coincides with the northern boundary of some deciduous trees, mainly the hazel, because for part of the year nutcrackers live on hazel nuts and other deciduous fruits.

the environs of towns and villages. Adaptability to new environments is a highly valuable quality: a species which succeeds in utilizing a new environment can expand. Because they have adjusted to an urban environment, the collared dove and black redstart have expanded beyond their original distribution areas in Asia and the Mediterranean countries.

Stratification and the relatively stable environment (with more constant temperature, humidity and wind conditions than in other environments on dry land) give woods and forests a rich assortment of animal and birdlife. An abundant plant supply in the form of seeds, fruit, leaves and wood leads to a multiplicity and complexity of food chains. The primary consumers – insects, seed-eating birds, mice, etc. – feed on the plants or producers. The creatures which in turn feed on the primary consumers, such as predatory insects and insect-eating birds, are secondary consumers. The food chain can then have a third or fourth link, and so on, until at the very end are birds of prey and predatory animals. Many species are consumers at more than one stage or level. The nuthatch, for instance, is a primary consumer of hazel nuts, a secondary consumer of herbivorous insects and a tertiary consumer of the eggs of insect-eating birds. The leaves, pine needles, twigs

Degrading organisms

and dead animals which fall to the ground are invaded by bacteria, fungi and other degrading organisms which feed on the organic substances present. Eventually soil is formed and new plants grow. In this way the forest is an ecosystem in which all organisms are interdependent.

Field identification and the outward structure of birds

Field identification has come a long way in the past few decades but is still developing. When some currently accepted 'facts' are reconsidered in the light of new knowledge, there is improvement in our ability to identify certain species correctly.

Many qualities or attitudes are useful to a field ornithologist – interest, experience, patience and self-criticism. But there is one which I would particularly like to emphasize – *looking at birds*, really *watching* and listening to even the most common species. Knowledge of the variations in the appearance, behaviour, haunts and notes of the most common species is often vitally important when identifying a rarer one. When seen in its usual surroundings under good conditions, a species may be easily recognizable. But one should observe the numerous small details of appearance and behaviour in all birds which cannot be included in this small field guide. Collect information of this kind, mainly noting deviations from the norm, until a mass of reference material is acquired. Then, when confronted with an unknown bird, for instance a non-European thrush, one can answer the following questions about the song thrush. Can the sides of its belly be plain? Can it show traces of rings around the eyes? How coarse are its facial markings? How does the colour of its upper parts change in bright sunshine? How does it move on the ground? How does it fly? And so on. An essential ingredient of birdwatching is to make careful field notes of the characteristics observed. This should even be done with birds one recognizes, and certainly for those one cannot identify. A note should be made of characteristics such as behaviour, habitat, accompanying birds, circumstances, the time of observation and, for more unusual species, the names of any co-observers. Sketching the bird also really forces a close study.

When identifying a bird in its natural environment, it may of course be no more than a particular detail or a series of characteristics and circumstances that can make a conclusion. The main observations, however, are the bird's appearance, behaviour, call and habitat. Take into account, too, the weather locally and over Europe as a whole and the season of the year.

Plumage

When studying a bird's appearance, a knowledge of bird morphology and of the relevant terminology is often essential. The main points

13

Third primary of long-eared owl

Third primary of buzzard

distinguishing birds from other classes of animals are their plumage and their ability to fly.

Basically there are two kinds of feathers: down and contour. But there are also a number of intermediate forms. Contour feathers can be divided into 1) flight and tail feathers and 2) body feathers. The latter combine to form a continuous protective surface with the down as an underlying, heat-insulating layer. The wing feathers which, together with the tail, are the most important for flying are the primaries and secondaries, according to their position on the 'hand' (primaries) and 'arm' (secondaries) of the wing. The primaries of perching birds, like their secondaries, number usually nine or 10. The bastard-wing comprises three feathers fastened to the counterpart of the human thumb. In certain wing positions it prevents unfavourable aerodynamic conditions ('stall') developing on top of the wing. The tail feathers, usually between 10 and 12 in perching birds, are vital for balance and steering. The feathers are positioned in certain tracts over the body, forming more or less distinct portions of the bird's outward shape. When describing plumage, note these areas first. (See the picture opposite.)

Feathers vary a great deal from one species to another, because they have been developed to cope with different environments and living conditions. For example, the deeply emarginated outer primaries of birds of prey are a modification for gliding, and the soft feathers of owls make their flight almost noiseless, allowing them to take rodents by surprise.

Moulting

The state of its feathers is crucial to a bird's survival, so plumage must be constantly maintained. Worn and ragged feathers impair flying ability and with it the ability to find food, escape from enemies and reduce the resistance

14

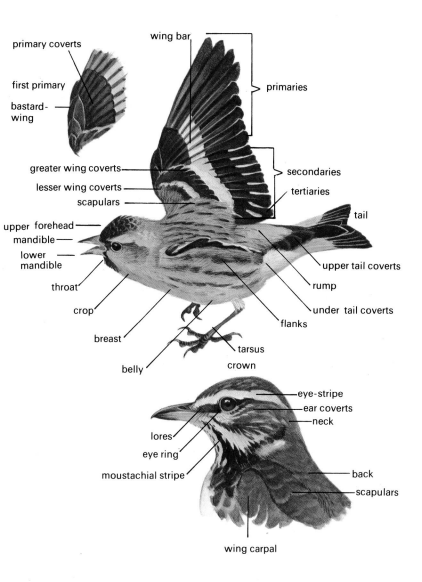

to cold and water. Feathers constantly deteriorate under strain, and have to be replaced at regular intervals. This process – moulting – occurs fairly regularly and follows particular – often complicated – sequences. Both the sequence and the number of plumage changes per year vary from one family to another and even between species of the same family. With few exceptions wing and tail feathers change once a year, while in addition perching birds also change their body plumage. This change is a complete

Moulting starling.
Juvenile plumage being
replaced by an adult one
(winter dress)

moult. Many species change their body feathers twice a year, some also change their tertiaries and some their tail feathers twice yearly. The willow warbler is one of the few to change body, wing and tail feathers completely twice a year.

When moulting occurs, and how long it takes, vary greatly from one species to another. Many start to moult after the breeding season. However, feather change demands extra energy, and birds must have abundant food supplies before and during their moult. Species which migrate over long distances need a completely grown set of feathers while they are on the move. Many of these insect-eating long-distance migrants depend on food supplies which dwindle rapidly during late summer. As a result they may not have time to complete their moult between the end of the breeding season and the beginning of migration. In this case they may defer moulting until reaching the wintering area or even commence moulting at a stop-over en route.

The need for a complete and efficient set of feathers varies. Ducks, for

16

example, swim or dive for their food and may moult enough feathers to become flightless, while birds of prey depend on flying for their livelihood. The sparrowhawk's mate can start to moult in the nest because he will supply her with food while she is on the nest. Local circumstances can affect moult, causing two individuals of the same species to look very different. Different geographical populations and races living in different climatic conditions may also display such differences. But in all cases the moulting process is devised so as not to impair the ability to obtain food and to fly.

Different dresses

Perching birds have two or three principal plumages. The first real one is the juvenile or immature plumage. In the newly hatched nestling it is usually preceded by a down covering. The next plumage comes from a change of body feathers, often as early as the late summer or autumn of the same year. The bird then looks more or less the same as an adult. In species which shed their body feathers twice yearly, one can sometimes see a special winter plumage and a special breeding plumage, for example, in the pied flycatcher. In larger species, including some perching birds, adult plumage is acquired gradually over several years. The transitional forms between juvenile and adult are sub-adult plumages. In many predatory species a bird will wear more than two generations of feathers at the same time.

Perching birds which do not change into a special breeding plumage show a different kind of colour change. Redstarts, linnets and bramblings, for example, have an inconspicuous winter plumage and a brighter coloured summer plumage even though they do not change their body feathers more

juvenile   winter   summer

Plumage changes in the pied flycatcher

Abrasion in the redstart

autumn   spring

than once a year. This comes after the breeding season, and the feathers which then appear have a pale outer part called a fringe or tip. Because these fringes contain less pigment, they are less resistant to wear, and when worn off, reveal the colourful lower part of the feather. This process is called abrasion.

Many species, such as thrushes and warblers, have only one distinguishable adult dress, and plumage wear and tear is usually unimportant as a factor in colour change (cf. the redstart).

While studying colouring and patterns, therefore, note these variations in the individual bird: age, moult phase, and wear and tear.

Great tit   ♂   ♀

In addition to individual variations there are differences between members of the same species (apart, too, from the differences between the sexes). These are obvious in many birds of prey, but few among perching birds. For example, study closely a flock of fieldfares or greenfinches and note the striking individual differences even in a fairly uniform species; all great tits look alike at first sight, but there can be wide colour differences between individuals, especially between male and female. In the redpoll, most warblers and some buntings, individual variations can be so great that field recognition is difficult. The great differences between redpolls and willow warblers, for example, are often geographical in origin: they are differences between variously evolved races.

Many other circumstances can also affect our conception of a bird's colour and patterning: contrasts, translucency, back lighting or bright sunshine. This happens particularly when groups must be identified from afar, like birds of prey.

Shape and size

Shape and size are decisive in the field recognition of certain species. For instance, the lesser spotted and great spotted woodpecker are hard to tell apart except for their size. On the other hand this can often be very difficult to judge. Always try to make a comparison with an accompanying bird whose size you already know. Posture and shape can cause a species to look larger or smaller than it actually is. A lesser spotted eagle, for instance, may seem to look much bigger and heavier than a buzzard, although there is only a slight difference between them. Mist, also, makes things look bigger than they really are.

Apart from the more obvious differences such as leg length and bill shape, there are a number of minor differences of posture and shape such as neck, tail and forehead angles and plumpness which are often useful recognition aids. Although body shape and posture vary depending on what the bird is doing, the small give-away angles making up the bird's 'personality' often remain. There can, however, be quite a difference in body shape between a resting and an active bird. A dust-bathing house sparrow looks like a grey, hairy bundle, while the same bird hopping about on the ground looks much longer and slimmer. The robin, normally plump and round-bellied, can sometimes look rather gaunt after the exertions of feeding its brood and when its plumage has become shabby (see p. 20). Birds fluff their feathers in cold weather, and the young tend to be rounder or 'fluffier' than their elders. Then again, the young of predator species often have broader wings than their parents.

Robin

autumn

summer

Calls and song

The more one studies and learns about birds, the more important their calls become for recognition purposes. The different notes of the species are the observer's principal means of discovery and identification, especially where the view is restricted in forests, woods and where migrants visit. A number of related species such as willow warbler and chiffchaff, icterine warbler and melodious warbler, and treecreepers and short-toed treecreepers can only be sorted out by their calls. The different notes of each species have a special function or significance to its members. Calls can be grouped according to function, but the boundaries between groups are flexible. The following is only a rough guide: song (real song and sub-song), summoning call, contact call, warning call and other calls of unknown function.

In many cases the song only practised by the male of the species serves a number of purposes. Perching bird species with a very loud and pure song often cover such extensive areas that all breeding activities are conducted within the boundaries: the pied flycatcher and the chaffinch are in this category. By singing from a strategic position in his territory, the male announces that the area is occupied and that, if he is alone, he is looking for a mate.

The song has varying degrees of feeling or intensity. Outside the breeding season, and mainly just before it begins, the male, and also the female in some cases, can produce an uninspired, restrained song. Many territorial species stake out a territory in their wintering places and even in temporary stopping places along their migration routes, when they often produce a feeble version of their song. Young birds, for example, chiffchaff and willow warbler, also practise a type of sub-song during late summer and autumn.

The distinction and significance of the various summoning and contact calls are sometimes unclear. In many species one can distinguish a direct contact call such as the coal tit's 'tsi' notes and the siskin's rough flight note. In these species the contact note keeps the flock close together and in touch. A bird emitting a louder and clearer summoning call is usually trying to establish contact over a greater distance. A stray redpoll invariably gives a summoning 'djuiii'. In some species warning and summoning calls merge, or are combined according to mood, while in others they are completely separate. Some species have a whole repertoire of contact and summoning calls, just as others may combine them. Larger species, such as birds of prey and owls, have various other notes, used, for example, in connexion with mating, or the delivery of prey. All young birds fed by their parents also have suppliant notes to indicate their whereabouts and hunger.

Notes are as variable as appearances. Redwings, willow warblers and linnets often display considerable geographical and individual song variations. Listening to and writing down the notes even of identified species is an important way to improve your knowledge of field ornithology.

Behaviour, habitat and distribution

Observing the behaviour or general 'deportment' is a good way of deciding to which family a bird belongs. Many relatively similar species differ behaviourally. Observe how the bird flies and looks for food, whether it is in a group or alone, whether it prefers the ground or a tree, and if so, which part of the tree. The garden warbler and nightingale look somewhat alike but can be told apart by their completely different behaviour, and a blackbird hops along the ground while the starling walks or runs. Movement pattern can determine the general impression; the silhouette on the wing can be identified by the speed of wing movements and trajectory of flight. The pattern and sequence of movements play an especially important role in recognizing birds of prey.

A bird often instinctively frequents a small area of the countryside which is its particular 'niche' in the ecosystem; this is a characteristic of every species. A greyish coloured tit with a black cap, seen in Scandinavia, will probably be a marsh tit if it is in deciduous woodland and a willow tit in coniferous woodland. Geographical distribution is also an important clue to recognition, although it is not the only evidence. The different distribution areas of the species can nevertheless be very useful evidence when trying to distinguish, for example, between the nightingale and the thrush nightingale. In field recognition, therefore, consider the probability in relation to the area in which the species normally occurs. But it takes more powerful documentation and knowledge to identify a bird in an area where it is not normally encountered. The time of year the observation is made should also be taken into account.

Next to the description of each species in this book is a map showing its distribution. Population density varies widely, so remember that certain species are exceedingly rare or entirely lacking in large parts of their distribution area. Breeding areas are generally more constant than wintering areas, which vary from year to year. Also, some species, such as the collared dove and rosefinch, are expanding fast, while others are contracting.

Blue: nests, summer visitor only

Blue and shading: nests and winters

Shading: winter visitor

Broken line: irregular winter visitor

Spruce cones worked on by:

Tail feathers removed by:

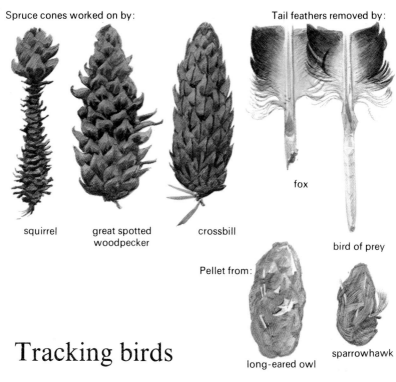

squirrel

great spotted
woodpecker

crossbill

fox

bird of prey

Pellet from:

long-eared owl

sparrowhawk

Tracking birds

Birds leave less of a trail than mammals, but even traces can be informative.
Grouse droppings, for example, help to establish the presence of these
species in an area. Many birds, especially birds of prey and owls, regurgi-
tate and discard indigestible food in the form of pellets. Cones worked on
by great spotted woodpeckers and crossbills are easy to find. If feathers are
torn out instead of bitten off, it shows that a victim has been taken by a bird
of prey.

Droppings of:

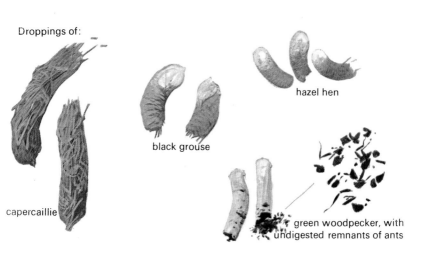

hazel hen

black grouse

capercaillie

green woodpecker, with
undigested remnants of ants

Silhouettes of birds of prey

Kite

Marsh harrier

Goshawk

Peregrine

Short-toed eagle

hovering

Buzzard

Lesser spotted eagle

Birds of Prey   *Falconiformes*

Feed on living animals (including birds), insects and carrion. Good flying technique, strong curved beaks and powerful feet and talons are ideal for catching and eating living prey. Most species circle, using rising columns of warm air and the upward airstreams on mountainsides and forest edges. Field identification is complicated by great colour and size variations within the same species. Females are noticeably larger than males. Adult plumage is often acquired by stages, which can take up to three or four years in the larger species. The colour and size of a lone bird outlined against the sky can be hard to judge, and silhouette, pattern of movement and general behaviour are therefore important characteristics. The species included here breed mainly in European woodland and forest areas, but many are also found in more open country, together with several other predatory species. Classification of the group to which a particular individual belongs is the first step towards reliable identification. There are two sub-orders: falcons (Falcones) and Accipitres, divided into kites, vultures, short-toed eagles, harriers, hawks, buzzards, eagles and the osprey.

Short-toed eagle

light phase

dark phase

Short-toed eagle

Short-toed eagle *Circaetus gallicus*

63–69 cm
wing span 190 cm approx.

Larger than the lesser spotted eagle and on the wing looks fairly light because of its pale underparts and gentle, 'elastic' wing movements. Can be confused with the osprey, which is closely attached to fresh water but has a dark carpal patch and, usually, darker secondaries underneath its wings. When viewed head on during circling flight, has more of a gull's wing angle. Pale buzzards are similar in colour but can be distinguished by their dark carpal marking. The head colour and markings vary; the underparts of some individuals are uniformly light. Hovers with its legs dangling. The short-toed eagle is absent from Britain and rare in the northern part of its distribution, breeding in open deciduous woodland. Lives mainly on reptiles and prefers wooded areas close to open and sunlit ground such as heaths.

Blackbird   ♂

Sparrowhawk   *Accipiter nisus*   28–38 cm   wing span 60–75 cm

Broad blunt wings and a long tail profile make it similar only to the goshawk. The female is similar in size to the male goshawk. In flight, however, it has a more slender profile, longer tail and less conspicuous under-tail coverts. When perched, shows greyish brown instead of grey upper parts, thinner legs and strikingly square-ended tail. Young birds have brownish red feather edges on their upper parts and wider belly markings, also touched with brownish red. In its breeding grounds often emits a persistent, monotonous 'chee-chee-chee ...', and during display flight also produces a tern-like rattling sound. Found in most woodlands, and in open country with isolated clumps of trees. Lives mainly on small birds caught on the wing after a short hectic chase. Its presence often betrayed by warning cries of small birds.

Goshawk   *Accipiter gentilis*   48–61 cm   wing span 98–117 cm

Has a shorter tail than the sparrowhawk and blunter wings than a falcon. In flight, glides like the sparrowhawk with semi-retracted wings between bursts of rapid wing beats, although these are slower than the sparrowhawk's and more reminiscent of a falcon. Occasionally circles, but most often its powerful pigeon-like build is seen hunting through the trees on the forest's edge. Flies close to the ground in more open country. Unlike the sparrowhawk, sometimes sits on a fence post or an exposed branch. Requires large continuous wooded areas (deciduous or coniferous) and is thus rare in Britain. Lives on small mammals and birds as big as woodpigeons.

Sparrowhawk

Goshawk

Sparrowhawk

♂ ♀

♀

♀

♂

juvenile

Goshawk

Black kite   *Milvus migrans*   56 cm   wing span 104–145 cm

A beautifully proportioned flight silhouette, more compact than the kite. Slimmer than the buzzard but differs in the greater length and shallower fork of its tail, pale diagonal stripes on top of its wings and lazier, often playfully swinging flight. Circles with wings flat, unlike the marsh harrier and the buzzard, which hold theirs in a V-shape (see p. 30). Underparts, throat and head of young birds have conspicuous pale patches, and underneath their wings are paler at the base of the primaries. Notes include a gull-like screech, sometimes followed by a chattering noise, and a buzzard-like mewing. The various races occur everywhere in the Old World, and are the most often observed and most conspicuous of all predators. Apart from the Mediterranean, breeds in European woodland or forest close to rivers. Eats living and dead fish, carrion and, especially further south, refuse in towns and villages. Rare wanderer to Britain.

Kite   *Milvus milvus*   61 cm   wing span 142–153 cm

A refined version of the black kite: has a long, deeply forked tail, capriciously manoeuvred at different angles, and the easy movement of its slender wings makes for a strikingly elegant flight. Circles with wings flat or slightly bowed. Differs from the black kite in its rust-red tail with a deep fork. The more pronounced rust-red and contrasting white patches underneath its wings are good field characteristics. Young birds have less deeply forked tails, with sand-coloured underparts and tail. Translucent inner primaries often make the wings look more angular than the black kite's. In their breeding grounds kites emit a variable, rather shrill neighing sound, 'hiah-hi-hi-hi-hi-hi-hiah', and also have a mewing note, softer and thinner than the buzzard's. Found in undulating, often hilly country where areas of old deciduous woodland are intermingled with open fields or grassland. In winter often collect in flocks at dusk to spend the night in woods or copses. They hunt across open country and live on small rodents, birds, insects and also carrion and refuse, particularly during the autumn and winter. Sometimes they have been seen to steal prey from other birds, like rooks and crows. In Britain, rare vagrant except in Wales, where there is a small breeding population.

Black kite

Kite

Black kite

Kite

Honey buzzard *Pernis apivorus*

51–58 cm
wing span 117–125 cm

In flight is not very different from the buzzard. The colour and patterning vary a great deal. Important marking differences from the buzzard are the tail bars and heavier pattern patches underneath the wings, although not in juvenile birds. When circling, the silhouette has a thinner head held forward, and a longer tail, which also has rounder corners. When gliding, note its rounded tail and less retracted wings with straight trailing edges. Juveniles may be confused with buzzards, because in autumn they often have a buzzard-like short, but rounded tail. Markings are varied but contrasting dark secondaries underneath and a pale head with a dark 'highwayman's mask' are frequent characteristics. Leads a secluded life in deciduous or mixed forest and never sits in the open like the buzzard. Lives mainly on the larvae and chrysalids of wasps and bumble bees, but also devours other insects and, occasionally, berries. Migrates to tropical Africa in August or September, returning in May.

Buzzard *Buteo buteo*

51–56 cm   wing span 114–133 cm

Easily confused with the honey buzzard, but has a heavier look, holds its wings more stiffly and makes a more compact, dumpy impression, especially when gliding. Extremely variable colour, but markings differ from the honey buzzard's. The buzzard usually circles with V-shaped wings, but the honey buzzard with wings horizontal or slightly cupped. Has a rounder, thicker head, shorter, wider tail and, usually, wider wing bases. The palest buzzards are almost completely white underneath and can be confused with pale individuals of the much larger short-toed eagle but have a dark, crescent-shaped carpal marking. The rough-legged buzzard, which breeds in northernmost Scandinavia but is seen further south in winter, has a white tail ending in a wide black bar, is normally pale in colour and has large, heavily marked carpal patches underneath. The *vulpinus* race of the buzzard, which is larger, has a paler, brick-coloured tail and, as a rule, a clearer dark carpal patch underneath, breeds in north-east Scandinavia and Siberia and is a migrant elsewhere. The buzzard's commonest note is a mewing, whistling 'pieeeh'. Prefers breeding in wooded areas adjoining open ground or moorland where it hunts for insects, worms, nestlings, reptiles and small rodents.

Honey buzzard

Buzzard

Honey buzzard

Buzzard

pale phase

Lesser spotted eagle   *Aquila pomarina*

A small, well-proportioned eagle with long, rectangular wings. Like the spotted eagle, holds its wings downwards or else with the primaries slightly cupped when circling or gliding. (The honey buzzard also sometimes droops its wings.) There is often a striking pale patch near the base of the inner primaries and also on the upper part of the rump. Older birds often have conspicuous yellow-brown coverts on the tops of their wings. It is often very hard to separate the two spotted eagle species. Variations in colour, pattern, moult phase and observation circumstances make some individuals of both species very difficult, perhaps impossible, to identify. As a general rule the lesser spotted eagle when seen from below has a slight contrast between its paler wing coverts and somewhat darker wing feathers, but in the larger species this is reversed. The lesser spotted eagle is normally smaller, of a lighter and slightly slimmer build, with more distinct pale patches on the tops of its wings confined to the inner primaries. Often sits like a buzzard on posts and similar observation points, or slightly elevated ground. Relatively common in its breeding areas, which are extensive woodlands or forest bordering on open meadows and wetlands in eastern Europe. It is a very rare vagrant to western Europe. Lives on small mammals, frogs and insects.

Spotted eagle   *Aquila clanga*   62–74 cm   wing span 158–182 cm

Sometimes very hard to distinguish from the lesser spotted eagle. Both species differ from other raptors by, among other things, their wing posture (see above). Generally darker than the lesser species, the pale area at the base of the primaries is formed at the top by pale feather vanes and extends to the front edge of the wing (see above). The patches are usually conspicuous underneath, which they are not in the lesser species. The spotted eagle may wander to Scandinavian countries during winter but is exceedingly rare elsewhere in western Europe. Young white-tailed eagles are bigger, have more wedge-shaped tails, longer and slimmer necks, thicker beaks, keep their wings horizontal and always have pale markings in their 'armpits'. Spotted eagles breed in large wooded areas close to water but are far less numerous than the lesser spotted eagle. They eat small mammals, frogs and carrion.

Lesser spotted eagle

Spotted eagle

Lesser spotted eagle
juvenile

adult

Lesser spotted eagle

adult

juvenile

juvenile

Spotted eagle

Black kite

Kite

Lesser spotted eagle
juvenile

adult

Lesser spotted eagle

Spotted eagle adult

colour phases

Buzzard

colour phases

Honey buzzard

Capercaillie ♂   Black grouse ♂

Capercaillie   *Tetrao urogallus*   ♂ 86 cm   ♀ 62 cm

In flight the female differs from the female black grouse in size and by the rounder shape and brighter red of her tail. During the breeding season, from the end of March, cocks assemble at dusk to begin their courtship at crack of dawn. This continues on the ground and sometimes in trees. The display call, performed in about seven seconds, consists of beak clickings followed by a cork-like pop and, finally, a quacking sound. The bird's presence is often revealed by its droppings (see p. 23). It is a typical northern woodland bird and prefers to live among old conifers, preferably pines, and small bog patches with abundant berries. Feeds on pine needles, but also eats aspen leaves and, in winter, berries.

Black grouse   *Lyrurus tetrix*   ♂ 53 cm   ♀ 41 cm

The female's rapid flight makes her slightly forked tail and light wing-bars hard to spot. During the spring particularly, black grouse go through their courtship rituals ('leks') at dawn in groups of varying size assembled at regular display grounds in bogs, fields or ice-covered lakes, and after sunrise they often move to a treetop. The extraordinary cooing of the cock birds is like a distant ululation as dawn rises over their breeding grounds. This is interspersed with an explosive 'choo-ish'. Black grouse live on seeds and buds from the birch and other trees and on various berries and shoots, while the chicks also eat large quantities of insects. More widespread than the capercaillie, prefers more open country where fields and meadows alternate with patches of woodland.

Capercaillie

Black grouse

courtship

♀

♂

Capercaillie

♀

♂

Black grouse

Woodcock

Hazel hen *Tetrastes bonasia* 35–36 cm

A typical northeastern woodland bird, seen throughout the year in small groups in dark woods, mainly mixed woodland. Has a special predilection for damp valleys and ravines flanking small streams with alder and birch trees and a plentiful supply of berries. All one usually manages to see of a family is a few grey, black and white-edged tails disappearing quickly into the darkness of the trees, followed by the sound of gentle, rhythmic wing beats. Unlike the black grouse and capercaillie, they do not fly very far when startled, and often, when repeatedly approached, perch close to a tree trunk. Its presence is revealed by needle-sharp whistlings, similar to the song of a goldcrest or treecreeper. Southern races are more brownish red. Rarely seen outside the breeding range and never recorded in Britain.

Woodcock *Scolopax rusticola* 34 cm

Best known for its 'roding', a display flight at dusk during spring and, if there is a second brood, well into summer. Then it flies rapidly and jerkily along a special regular route, emitting a series of hoarse croaks followed by a loud, explosive creaking sound. In flight it also produces a rapid 'egh-egh-egh'. If, during summer, a woodcock is flushed near an overgrown bog, two or three others will then follow the hen and her brood. The young can already fly short distances when they are no more than 10 days old. The frightened bird will zig-zag between the trees, with slightly floppy wing movements, making a clapping sound as it climbs. Larger than the various snipe species, its wing movements are slower and its plumage far more rufous. Breeds in marshy areas of woods or forests, in ponds, muddy-banked streams or lakesides. Lives on worms and insects probed from mud and dead leaves with its bill.

Hazel hen

Woodcock

Hazel hen

Woodcock

Woodpigeon   *Columba palumbus*   41 cm

Always easily recognized by the white wing and throat markings. In silhouette looks heavier when flying, is deeper in the chest and has a longer tail than the stock dove. The wings clap loudly during take-off and landing. Its 'song' is a muffled, blowing 'who-hoo-hoo-hoohoo'; the actual number of syllables varies. The note has a desolate timbre resembling the hooting of an owl. In northern Europe it is mostly a shy, retiring bird, breeding mainly in spruce forests, but to the west and south fearlessly frequents urban parks as well as woods and farmland. Varied vegetarian diet, including clover, and often damages crops. During September and October they congregate in large flocks.

Stock dove   *Columba oenas*   33 cm

The stock dove is smaller than the woodpigeon. Its steadier and faster flight makes it look more evenly proportioned, with a shorter tail. Can be mistaken for a feral, or town, pigeon, but these lack the distinct black trailing wing edges. The male emits a very low pitched, rapidly repeated bisyllabic 'oo-oh, oo-oh, oo-oh ...' In courtship flights the bird displays like a town pigeon, with wings held in a V-shape. Its breeding ground depends mostly on the availability of suitable nesting holes in old trees, disused buildings, or nestboxes and thus is less widespread than the woodpigeon. Its diet is similar to the woodpigeon's.

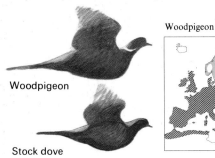

Woodpigeon

Stock dove

Woodpigeon

Stock dove

juvenile

Woodpigeon

Stock dove

Turtle dove

Turtle dove *Streptopelia turtur* 27 cm

When a turtle dove is flushed at close quarters, the markings on the fanned tail are outstanding. It often has a darting flight, somewhat like a high-speed butterfly, with shallow, flicking wing movements. In normal flight the tail markings are seldom visible, and the bronze back and short tail mark its difference from the collared dove. Young birds are more greyish-brown, without the distinctive neck patch. A common, noisy, but somewhat shy, breeding resident in cultivated land with hedges, scrub or open deciduous woods, and in large gardens. They often sit in pairs or small groups on telephone wires and in fields, but their presence is mostly revealed by their song, which is a gently purring continuous 'torr, torr ...' or 'turr ...', hence the name of the species. They feed on various plant seeds, buds and shoots.

Collared dove *Streptopelia decaocto* 31 cm

Distinguished from the turtle dove by its pale greyish brown colour, shape of the collar around its neck and, when taking off, by its tail markings. In flight has a longer tail and paler overall appearance and pale wings underneath. During the display flight, which resembles the turtle dove's, it parachutes down with wings bent slightly downwards and tail outstretched, conspicuously demonstrating the markings on the underside of its tail. Young birds have no collar and are greyer. The note is a rich 'coocoo, coo'. The collared dove originally came from Asia but has spread rapidly northwest in this century and is common in parks and gardens close to human settlement. Huge flocks will congregate in winter where there is spilled corn.

Turtle dove

Collared dove

Turtle dove

Collared dove

Eagle owl *Bubo bubo* 61–71 cm

Always makes a big and unmistakable impression. The great grey owl found in the north and east of Scandinavia and further eastwards is completely grey and has yellow, sometimes orange-red, eyes, while the Ural owl, of the north and east of Scandinavia, further east and in the Carpathians, is smaller and is basically light ochre with black eyes. In flight the eagle owl has a short tail, wide wings and rather stiff wing movements. The territorial call of the male is a resounding 'o-ho' or 'oh-au', while the female's similar note is about an octave higher. Around its breeding grounds it produces a variety of other noises during courtship and when delivering prey. It breeds in undisturbed woods, steep rocky areas or caves and lives on mammals and sometimes surprisingly large birds. Human intrusion and pollution have caused the population to fall disastrously in some parts of its range. Rarely ventures into western Europe.

Long-eared owl *Asio otus* 36 cm

Seated, can be distinguished from the tawny owl by its orange-red eyes and long 'ears'. Wing movements in flight are mechanically jerky and stiff but it is very agile among trees. On the wing it can be mistaken for a short-eared owl (*Asio flammeus*), but this species, which occurs on moorland and coastal marshes, has longer wings which, seen from below, usually have darker tips. The short-eared owl has hardly any 'ears', but has distinct dark eye patches and (unlike the long-eared owl) frequently sits on the ground. The barn owl (*Tyto alba*), closely associated with farmland, does not have streaked underparts or a dark carpal marking. The long-eared owl is largely nocturnal and also hunts at dusk and dawn but, unlike the short-eared owl, very rarely in broad daylight. The territorial calls of the male are a 'pooh' mechanically repeated at two or three second intervals. The female has a brighter and longer 'pouuuu'. When the young perch in surrounding trees, they report their positions with clear, plaintive whistlings, 'piee'. The long-eared owl nests in the abandoned nests of crows and birds of prey in woods or copses, but needs some open ground – glades, moor, marsh or farmland – for hunting. It feeds on small rodents and small passerine birds caught at their roosts.

Eagle owl

Long-eared owl

Eagle owl

Long-eared owl

Tawny owl   *Strix aluco*   38 cm

A nocturnal bird mostly seen towards daybreak. Even then hard to spot, as it sits close against a tree trunk. Distinguished from the long-eared owl by completely black eyes, which often have a sleepy, bleary look in the daytime. In its moth-like flight the wings look relatively short and rounded, and when gliding are held slightly downwards. Colour varies from rufous through brown to greyish. The male's territorial call is a mellifluous 'poohoo' followed by a vibrant 'poo-hoo'o'o'o'o'o'o'. Both sexes also emit a whining 'chee-witt'. Breeds in open mixed or deciduous woodland, often penetrating deep into towns. They like old trees in parkland or avenues for nesting cavities. Feeds on small rodents, birds, frogs and worms.

Tengmalm's owl   *Aegolius funereus*   26 cm

Tengmalm's owl, restricted to northern and eastern Europe, cannot be confused with any other woodland or forest owl. (The somewhat smaller and browner little owl, unlike Tengmalm's, is mostly seen in open, cultivated country.) A young Tengmalm's owl is predominantly chocolate-brown. The territorial call, mainly heard between January and April, is an unmistakable sequence of between three and seven hollow rattling glottal stops – 'po-po-po-po-po'. Pre-eminently nocturnal, Tengmalm's owl is seldom seen, although relatively common and often heard. Its principal food is small rodents. In some years it makes invasion-like migrations to places outside its normal area but is a very rare visitor to countries as far west as Britain. Breeds in the abandoned nests of black woodpeckers in tall coniferous or mixed woods.

Pygmy owl   *Glaucidium passerinum*   17 cm

Easily recognized because of its diminutive stature. Active during the day and, because it is not at all shy, easily spotted. Fond of sitting in the tops of spruces, and has a habit of jerking its tail. Its territorial call is a rhythmically repeated, somewhat bullfinch-like whistling, 'piuh'. Particularly during autumn and winter, it produces a rising whistling – 'chut, chut, chut, chit, chit, chit'. Breeds in dense spruce forests or mixed woodland, but in winter appears in deciduous woodland and gardens where there are many small birds. Small birds and rodents are its principal foods. Restricted to northern and eastern Europe.

Tawny owl

Tengmalm's owl

Pygmy owl

grey phase

rufous phase

Tawny owl

Tengmalm's owl

Pygmy owl

Cuckoo *Cuculus canorus*   34 cm

Most often seen in flight, when its silhouette resembles the kestrel's. In open country
flies fast and straight, although its wing beats are shallow, the wings not rising above
the body, and the head shape and posture give it a somewhat sagging profile. Differs
from the sparrowhawk in its pointed, not rounded, wings. Female looks like the male
except for a slight brown breast bar. The young have pale fringes on the feathers of
their upper parts, but the underparts, breast and throat included, are heavily barred
with a distinct white neck patch. They are usually darker than adults, of a basic iron
grey, although a reddish brown phase is quite common for them (and very occasionally the female). The number of syllables in the characteristic 'cuckoo' can vary.
When angered by the presence of a rival, the male makes a hoarse, scolding 'gock-
gock-gock-cheh-cheh-cheh'. The female's explosive, bubbling trill is reminiscent of
the whimbrel. Found in open scrub, farmland and woodland, and common in
extensive reed-beds and on moorland, where it parasitizes reed warblers and meadow
pipits. During high summer it is quieter and less in evidence. Adults leave on south-
ward migration in July – up to a month earlier than the young, which navigate to
Africa unassisted. Lives on insects, especially hairy 'woolly bear' caterpillars, which
many other species avoid. The cuckoo lays her eggs in various other insectivorous
birds' nests, and after hatching, the fledgling ejects all the other eggs or young from
the nest and is reared by its foster parents.

Nightjar *Caprimulgus europaeus*   27 cm

Silhouette in flight very similar to the cuckoo's, but is a nocturnal bird, and when
flushed from its daytime perch will often fly only a short distance before coming to
rest again on a thick branch. Only the male has white markings on wings and tail.
Presence mostly betrayed by the male's nocturnal courtship song, a purring or grass-
hopper-like buzzing which often alternates between two tones: 'rrrrrrrrrrrrrr ...'
This note can be maintained for hours, with only short pauses. Its flight call is a
nasal 'kru-ek'. During the breeding season it puts on a flight display; the male
claps his wings and flies with slow wing beats interspersed with glides on upraised
wings, revealing the white patches. Lives on insects caught on the wing, using its extremely wide mouth as a kind of net. Likes open wooded country, glades and felled
areas or moorland.

Cuckoo

Nightjar

48–49

juvenile   rufous phase

Cuckoo   ♂

♀

Nightjar   ♂

Roller *Coracias garrulus* 32 cm

Unmistakable at close quarters, but in flight may resemble a pigeon or crow. Its straight flight resembles the stock dove but the roller has a slimmer body, larger and more rounded wings (rather like a lapwing's) and a longer and strikingly thin tail. Telephone wires and overhead cables are among its favourite vantage points, from which it makes redstart-like sorties against large insects on the ground or in the air; in many places it is a characteristic roadside bird. On the breeding grounds the male puts on a flight display, sometimes accompanied by the female. He corkscrews high above the trees with jerky wing beats, before descending in a daring combination of zig-zags and turns, to an accompaniment of croakings. On other occasions, the commonest call is a metallic, resonant 'rack' or 'rack-ack'. Nests in hollow trees but because it needs open sunlight areas to hunt, it is also seen in thin woodlands and parks. Lives on beetles, grasshoppers, worms and young frogs. These large insects as food for birds are characteristic of the hot summers of east and south Europe, where the roller (an African migrant) summers. It is a rare vagrant elsewhere.

Hoopoe *Upupa epops* 28 cm

Despite its plumage contrasts, difficult to spot when sitting on the ground. In flight, it is a living fireworks display, not unlike a gigantic butterfly. It is an unforgettable experience to watch a hoopoe flopping and bouncing over a couple of fields and stone walls on its rounded wings, only to drop suddenly to earth and disappear. Crouches close to the ground when frightened and will not fly up until you are almost on top of it. Crest normally kept lowered, making the bird look small and slight while pecking at the ground. Its note is a hollow 'po-po-po' audible at long ranges and a hoarse, soft hissing 'ah-ah-ah'. Most common in warm cultivated landscapes, where well-lit woodland, parks and gardens alternate with pasture and arable land. Lives on insects and larvae extracted from clefts, hollows and soft ground with its long beak; for example, its diet includes beetle larvae living in livestock dung. An uncommon but regular migrant in southern Britain mostly occurring in April and May, occasionally remaining to breed.

Roller

Hoopoe

50–51

Roller

Hoopoe

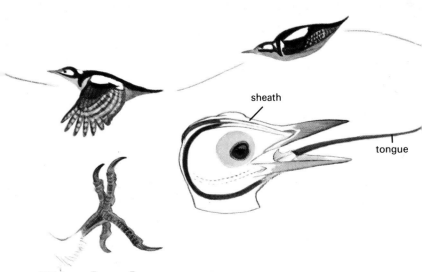

sheath

tongue

Woodpeckers *Picidae*

All woodpeckers, with the exception, in some respects, of the wryneck, are extremely well-adapted to the business of climbing vertically and pecking at tree trunks and branches. Their stout sharp beaks, feet ideal for climbing, and stiff pointed tail feathers support them. In addition, a woodpecker's tongue is long, with a stiff, barbed tip, and mucous secretions from special glands keep it permanently moist and sticky – the perfect instrument for reaching and capturing insects and their larvae in the tunnels and cavities under the bark. The long tongue is coiled around the skull, and the supporting bones (hyoids) are both fixed to the right nostril, so that the bird can breathe through the left one. Striking plumage, loud calls and the male's habit of 'drumming' on dry trunks and branches in spring are useful in locating and identifying the various species. Each of the following descriptions includes a diagram illustrating the approximate duration, form and loudness of its drumming, but the differences between the drumming styles of the species are more apparent in diagram form than they are in reality. Loudness, of course, varies according to distance and the type of wood on which the drumming is performed. In flight, wings are retracted between each burst of rapid wing beats, with an undulating flight trajectory.

Black woodpecker

♀

♂

Black woodpecker

Black woodpecker   *Dryocopus martius*   46 cm

No resemblance to other woodpeckers, but on the wing might be taken for a species of crow. Typical undulating flight only becomes conspicuous a few seconds before it comes to rest in a tree. Over longer distances wing movements are flappy and uneven, like a jay, as if it is treading water, counteracting every loss of height with a few extra-vigorous wing beats. In flight almost invariably emits a succession of piercing, truncated screeches, 'prii, prii, prii, prii, prii'. In spring also produces a 'clue, clue, clue, clue, clue', similar to the green woodpecker's note but more metallic. When perching it also has a prolonged metallic 'kliiiie'. For drumming it often selects the largest dry aspen or pine in the area. Its drum-rolls are incredibly loud. Breeds in pine or mixed forests where the trees have large trunks. Lives on various tree insects. Does not venture west of its breeding range.

Grey-headed woodpecker *Picus canus* 25 cm

The 'highwayman's mask', dark eye, relative or complete lack of red on the crown and greyer overall aspect distinguishes the grey-headed from the green woodpecker. During spring, however, the grey-headed is shy and withdrawn, mainly evidenced by its note. Mostly seen on the wing, and then displays a more slender head and bill profile, more graceful, cigar-shaped body and a longer tail than the green woodpecker. Compared with the note of the green the grey-headed's spring call seems almost feeble, a squeaky 'pi-eh, pi-eh, pue, pue, pue, pue .. pue ... pue'. This note is gentle and plaintive, with a despondent sag towards the end. Flight call a short 'kvick', reminiscent of the great spotted's. Drums more frequently than the green: weak but gathers strength towards the end. Breeds in the woods and forests of eastern and central Europe in thick-trunked deciduous trees. Further north, mostly seen in dense coniferous forests and woods interspersed with big aged aspen trees, in which it nearly always hollows out its nesting hole. During winter, unlike the green woodpecker, it sometimes visits farms and bird tables. Lives on insects and insect larvae dug from various deciduous trees. Does not venture west of its breeding range.

Green woodpecker *Picus viridis* 32 cm

Bigger than the grey-headed, and clearly identified at close quarters by its facial markings. The male especially has a brilliant yellow top to its rump. In flight often produces a rather shrill 'ku-ku-kuck'. Spring song is a loud, laughing, slightly falling 'clue-clue-clue-clue-clue-clue-clue', with a rounder, fuller tone than the grey-headed. This call gave rise to its old English name 'yaffle'. Sometimes emits a thinner 'pue-pue-pue-pue-pue-pue-pue', more like the grey-headed's call. Not an assiduous drummer, and its occasional performances, like the grey-headed's, are weak and shaky, lacking power and emphasis. Found in undulating open deciduous or mixed woodland, and in small groups of trees in cultivated landscapes. Looks for food on the ground more than in trees. Large holes in an ant hill show where it has plundered with its long sticky tongue.

Grey-headed woodpecker

Green woodpecker

♀ Grey-headed woodpecker ♂

♀

juvenile

Green woodpecker

♂

Great spotted woodpecker *Dendrocopos major* 23 cm

The commonest of the spotted woodpeckers. Similar in appearance to the white-backed and middle spotted. The young have a red crown. In late summer, older bird's ageing plumage often turns very dark greyish brown. The Syrian woodpecker, primarily a southeast European species, has recently spread northwards. It is very similar to the great spotted, except for differently patterned black head bars. Frequently emits a metallic 'kuck' or 'kick', but when annoyed the note is repeated with chattering rapidity, sometimes accelerating and turning into a vibrant dry rattling. Its drumming, usually six or seven strokes, is much faster than others of the species. A drum-roll rarely lasts for more than a second. Catholic in habitat choice but seems to need deciduous trees for nesting. Feeds its young mainly on insects and their larvae, but eats seeds and nuts in autumn and winter. Also eats food put out on bird tables, and in summer eggs and nestlings of other woodland birds. Food shortages lead to mass emigration from the Scandinavian countries, and some reach the east coast of Britain.

1 sec. 2

White-backed woodpecker *Dendrocopos leucotos* 25 cm

The biggest of the spotteds, looking heavier than the great spotted. The size of the white bars across the back varies considerably between individuals. Young birds have a red crown. The commonest note, 'kerk', is softer and lower pitched than the great spotted's. When annoyed, produces a rattling, grating 'prrrrrrrrrr'. The difference between the drum-rolls of the two species is a reliable clue for locating white-backed woodpeckers among drumming great spotted's. The three-toed woodpecker, which breeds in coniferous forests in northern Scandinavia and in the mountain forests of central Europe, has a drum-roll which may last for over a second but is more like the black woodpecker's in form. The white-backed frequents old woodland and forests with decayed and fallen deciduous trees. Unlike the great spotted, it often sits close to the ground digging out insect larvae. An eastern European bird, never recorded in Britain.

1 sec. 2

Great spotted woodpecker

White-backed woodpecker

Syrian woodpecker ♂

♀

♂

Great spotted
woodpecker

juvenile
Great spotted
woodpecker

♀

♂

White-backed woodpecker

Middle spotted woodpecker *Dendrocopos medius* 22 cm

Differs from the great spotted in smaller size, completely red crown, incompleteness of cheek stripes and streaked underparts. More restless than its larger relative. Call similar in tone to the great spotted but more regularly repeated in a 'kik-kik-kik-kik'. Very seldom drums in spring, but has mewing similar to the spring cries of the grey-headed and green woodpeckers. This note is repeated at somewhat irregular intervals: 'kveh, kveh, kveh, kveh ... kveh, kveh ... kveh'. Lives on various insects in deciduous woods with large numbers of oak trees. Despite its proximity on the continent, never recorded in Britain.

Lesser spotted woodpecker *Dendrocopos minor* 14.5 cm

Immediately distinguishable from other woodpeckers because it is smaller, and lacks red traces beneath, giving a striking black-and-white impression. Often jumps way out on small branches, but prefers to sit parallel to the branch – typical of woodpeckers. Advertises its presence with a 'kick' and a rather wryneck-like 'ki-ki-ki-ki-ki-ki-ki'. In spring often drums on telephone poles like the great spotted, although with a softer, higher pitched and more prolonged sound usually lasting for over a second, often rapidly repeated twice with a short hiatus in the middle. Breeds in deciduous or mixed woodland, often by water. Looks for its insect food among the branches of both dead and live trees.

```
           1 sec.  2      3
 llllllll llllllll
```

Wryneck *Jynx torquilla* 16.5 cm

Distinctly unlike other woodpecker species. Indeed, with its reptilian body elongation, rather sluggish movements and reticent habits it is not really like any other bird. Glides for long distances with wings retracted on its shallowly undulating flight. Arriving on its breeding grounds in May, advertises its presence mainly by its monotonously plaintive or squeaky note, 'tue-tue-tue ...' liable to be confused with that of the lesser spotted woodpecker. Breeds in open, deciduous or mixed woodland, orchards, parks and gardens. Builds in natural hollows and tree cavities or in nesting boxes. Lives mainly on ants. Now reduced to occurrences on migration in Britain.

Middle spotted woodpecker   Lesser spotted woodpecker   Wryneck

Middle spotted
woodpecker ♂

Lesser spotted
woodpecker ♀ ♂

Wryneck

Perching birds Order *Passeriformes*

The largest order in total membership and number of species. Shape, size and living habit vary a great deal, but one common feature is the combination of three forward and one rear pointing toes. Many are forest or woodland birds. Classification by family helps identify perching birds, which are divided as follows:

Larks (*Alaudidae*) predominantly mottled brown, adapted to life on the ground, and with a long, usually straight, rear claw. Principal diet: seeds, fresh grass shoots and varying quotas of insects. The woodlark, the only lark regularly occurring and breeding in forest or woodland, lives mainly on insects. **Swallows** (*Hirundinidae*) aerial-feeding insect-eaters, occasionally seen in woodland but rarely breeding there. **Wagtails** and **pipits** (*Motacillidae*) graceful and long-legged with an elegant posture and relatively long tails. Live mainly on the ground, and feed almost exclusively on insects. **Shrikes** (*Laniidae*) perching birds with colourful or contrasting plumage, frequenting woodland margins or glades. Feed on insects, small rodents and birds, hence the predatory bill. **Orioles** (*Oriolidae*) the only European representative of this family, the golden oriole, eats insects, fruit and berries. **Starlings** (*Sturnidae*) short-tailed and gregarious, live on insects, snails, worms, berries and fruit, probed from loose soil. **Crows** (*Corvidae*) largest of the perching birds. Mostly black, with grey or white markings. Seen in most habitats and are mainly omnivores. Use their stout bills to open eggs, take nestlings, kill small animals, dismember car-

Red-backed shrike

Starling

Crow

rion and dig up worms. **Dippers** (*Cinclidae*) river birds. **Wrens** (*Troglodytidae*) are the sole European representatives of a family which is very extensive in North America. Live on small invertebrates. **Accentors** (*Prunellidae*) resemble both sparrows and warblers and live mainly on vegetable food. The *Muscicapidae* family

Wren

is divided into the sub-families **warblers** (*Sylviinae*) (p. 74), **flycatchers** (*Muscicapinae*) (p. 75) and **thrushes** (*Turdinae*) (p. 75), which comprise thrushes, redstarts, robin and nightingales. **Bearded reedlings** (*Timaliinae*)

Warbler

Flycatcher

Thrush

Tit

Treecreeper

Finch

marshland birds, **penduline tits** (*Remizidae*) marshland birds, **tits** (*Paridae*): see p. 96. **Nuthatches** (*Sittidae*) specialize in climbing non-horizontal surfaces, but do not support themselves with their tails. The stout beak can crack hazel nuts, but they also eat insects and spiders. **Creepers** (*Certhiidae*) specialize in climbing trees, using their long bills to winkle out insects and larvae from crevices and cracks in tree bark. Long claws hook into the trunk and stiff tail feathers support them like woodpeckers. **Sparrows** (*Ploceidae*), **finches** (*Fringillidae*), **buntings** (*Emberizidae*): see p. 104.

Woodlark *Lullula arborea*   15 cm

Resembles a skylark but differs in its distinctly shorter tail and the light and dark markings on the leading wing edges. Looks rather bat-like in the air with wide wings, short tail and gently undulating flight. The young are 'scaly' on top, with pale-fringed feathers. The call 'luedloi' or 'tuetli-oit' is pleasantly soft and flutey. The soft melancholy song consists of repeated yodelling motifs, accelerating at one moment and then descending in pitch or suddenly halting. Usually frequents woodland clearings and hillsides with scattered trees. Lives mainly on insects and seeds.

Tree pipit *Anthus trivialis*   15 cm

The only European pipit regularly occurring in forest or woodland. On migration often rests with other pipits in open ground, and is then easily distinguished by its hoarse, rather buzzing call 'dzuz', unlike the sharper notes of the other pipits. It also produces a more delicate 'ziet'. The song is delivered during a soaring and then parachuting song flight which starts from the top of a tree. It is a succession of trills, accelerating and then slowing down as the bird loses height. Breeds in deciduous and mixed woodland clearings and lives mainly on insects.

Red-backed shrike *Lanius collurio*   17 cm

Like the other species in its family, scans its surroundings from a vantage point in search of prey. Females vary a great deal in colour and, like the young, can be confused with young woodchat shrikes (p. 64). Its variable song includes an abundance of imitative notes. The call is a forceful 'vehvv'. When disturbed closer to its nest it produces a harsher 'shack, shack' like a wheatear. Breeds in open country with dense bushes, and lives mainly on large insects. When food is in good supply it impales the surplus on thorns as a reserve for bad weather when there is a shortage of insects that only come out in the sun; other shrikes do the same, hence the name 'butcher bird'. Becoming scarce in Britain.

Woodlark

Tree pipit

Red-backed shrike

Woodlark

Tree pipit

juvenile

♀

♂

Red-backed shrike

Woodchat shrike *Lanius senator* 17 cm

Easily distinguished by its red crown and neck. Black and white markings make it appear dappled, especially in flight. The young differ from the young and females of the red-backed in their paler plumage and pale markings on shoulders, wings and rump. The female is drabber than the male with white markings at her bill base. A more melodious and varied song than the red-backed shrike's. Breeds in the same habitats as the red-backed shrike, but is predominantly a Mediterranean species, occurring in Britain irregularly as a passage migrant.

Lesser grey shrike *Lanius minor* 20 cm

Like a small great grey shrike, but with longer wings and shorter tail in proportion to its body. Has a black forehead, upright posture, contrast between white chin and pink breast, no white eyebrow markings and only slight white wing patches. The young have few markings on their bellies, differing from the young of the red-backed and woodchat. The song is more mellifluous and variable than the great grey shrike's. Occurs in open country with scattered trees and bushes. Rare vagrant to Britain.

Great grey shrike *Lanius excubitor* 24 cm

Striking appearance. Always sits openly on top of a bush, in a tree or on telephone wires. Can be mistaken for the lesser grey shrike, but at a distance its longer tail and horizontal posture make it obvious. At closer quarters, the absence of a black forehead, white crown and shoulder markings and strikingly short primaries are distinctive features. The white wing bars vary from a small patch at the base of the primaries to a thick bar across the wing. An undulating flight with successions of rapid wing beats alternating with completely closed wings. Its wing bars and the white tail marking are then clear from a considerable distance. Not much of a songster, mostly engaging in mousily shrill, vibrant trills and squeakings interspersed with a hoarse 'veck'. Other notes include a bright, ringing 'shrrree' and a prolonged nasal 'eeeh'. Lives on insects and small birds. Breeds in semi-open landscapes, often close to clearings, swamps or pasture.

Woodchat shrike

Lesser grey shrike

Great grey shrike

Woodchat shrike

juvenile

♂

Lesser grey shrike

♂

juvenile

Great grey shrike

Golden oriole *Oriolus oriolus* 24 cm

Despite its bright-coloured plumage, attracts attention mainly by its note. The male has an unmistakable, melancholy but fast and clear flutelike 'choo-oo-wee-oo'. Both sexes have a hoarse note somewhat like the jay. A shy graceful bird, about the size of a thrush, emerges from tree foliage in rapid starling-like flight, disappearing in gentle swoops to the next coppice. Its favourite haunt is high in the crowns of trees, where the male's yellow plumage disappears among the glitter of sunlight in the leaves. Year-old males resemble the females and do not acquire their black and yellow dress until they are about 15 months old. Various insects, larvae and beetles are their diet, which they sometimes catch on the wing. They build hammock-like nests in old deciduous woods and copses in open country.

Starling *Sturnus vulgaris* 21–25 cm

Cannot be confused with other birds. The blackbird has a longer tail and hops along, but the starling walks. Its thick stumpy body and alternating rapid wing beats and gliding on stiffly triangular wings make a special flight silhouette which can only be confused with the waxwing's (p. 72). The young are distinguished from other greyish brown birds by their short tail and rather amusing gait, a sort of elevated waddle. Starlings are highly gregarious, congregating in large flocks from midsummer onwards. Winter roosting flocks may be hundreds of thousands strong. A varied song featuring imitative sounds, chirrupy screechings, beak snappings and protracted bright whistlings with throat puffed out and wings flapping. During the breeding season lives mainly on insects and worms, but otherwise on berries, fruit and seeds. Starlings commonly nest in holes in old trees and will often build in nestboxes or under roof tiles.

Golden oriole

Starling

adult   spring

♀

♂

Golden oriole

adult autumn

juvenile

moulting

Starling

juvenile

Jay *Garrulus glandarius*   34 cm

A wary woodland bird often seen in autumn maintaining a shuttle between its 'home wood' and the surrounding oak trees, storing acorns for winter. In flight moves its round wings floppily in slow jerky progress. Glides along the edge of a wood or forest in deep swooping waves, showing pale blue wing patches and white rump. Its note is a harsh 'kreh', heard for a considerable distance and it also shares the buzzard's 'pieeeh'. Breeds in coniferous and mixed woodland and lives on insects and fruit, also regularly taking eggs and nestlings. Will visit bird tables, but unlike other members of the crow family seldom ventures from forests and woods.

Nutcracker *Nucifraga caryocatactes*   32 cm

A shy bird like the jay, mostly seen in autumn. Flight silhouette resembles the jay's, but with a shorter tail, slightly more stable trajectory and a thick bill. Its commonest call is a repeated croaking, brighter and noisier than the crow's. Also has a loud buzzing warning note, 'arrrrrr'. A coniferous forest bird preferring dense spruce woods with deciduous trees nearby, and it often perches on top of a spruce tree. The thin-billed Siberian race *macrorhynchus* occasionally invades areas further west, and Scandinavian birds, too, can emigrate as far west as Britain on a large scale during some years when food becomes short. Diet is pine seeds, nuts, fruit, insects and worms.

Magpie *Pica pica*   46 cm

Well known because of its distinctive appearance. It is primarily refuse that induces magpies to settle near houses and farms. They are very much on their guard near humans, and give an immediate warning at the approach of birds of prey, cats and other enemies. Apart from a hoarse croaking, they sometimes produce a soft, crowing song made up of fine whimperings and twitterings. Magpies mate for life. They are omnivores, and steal eggs and nestlings from other birds. Look for the conspicuous domed twiggy nest, high in a slender tree.

Jay

Nutcracker

Magpie

Jay

Nutcracker

Magpie

Raven   Carrion crow   Rook   Jackdaw

Carrion crow   *Corvus corone*   47 cm

The hooded and carrion crows are two races of the same species and can produce hybrids. Crows occur in most types of country and are common around towns and villages. They are much less gregarious than rooks and jackdaws. The croak call is more easily recognized than described. Omnivorous, and often visits rubbish tips. Takes the eggs and nestlings of other birds.

The hooded crow (*Corvus corone cornix*) has a grey back and underparts.

The carrion crow (*Corvus corone corone*) could be confused with the raven or rook, also black 'crows'. The rook frequents farmland and is a little slimmer, and the cheek patch at the base of its straight-sided bill is grey (although not in young birds). The raven is much bigger (about 65 cm) and has a stouter bill and a wedge-shaped tail.

Jackdaw   *Corvus monedula*   33 cm

Distinguished from other crows by its smallness, quicker movements and white eye iris. Skilled fliers, flocks will play aerial 'games', using wind and upcurrents, especially towards evening when they gather to spend the night together. Note is resonant and more melodious than the crow's. It varies considerably, but most often is a sharp, ringing 'tchah' or 'jack'. The male and female form a lifelong union, and often feed together. Breed in colonies in towns and villages, and in large woodland or farmland trees. In towns they will often build in church towers and other large buildings. They are less inclined than crows to rob the nests of other birds, and usually feed on plant and animal material in fields.

Hooded crow   Carrion crow   Jackdaw

Carrion crow

Hooded crow

Jackdaw

Wren   *Troglodytes troglodytes*   9.5 cm

Smallness, the almost permanently elevated tail and a voluble song are features common to all wrens, but behaviour, choice of habitat and, to some extent, colour vary greatly. In the British Isles it is a garden bird, sometimes breeding in nestboxes, and on a number of islands in the Atlantic. Always attracts attention by its song, astonishingly loud for its size, a persistent, excited warbling trill, high up on the scale. Prefers to be close to the ground, in thick bushes, brushwood or stone walls. Its size, brown colour and swift movements give it the appearance of a 'mouse bird'. Its call is a short, rolling 'zerr', often prolonged into a harsh chattering.

Dunnock   *Prunella modularis*   14.5 cm

A shy bird, preferring thickets, which seldom shows itself for more than a brief moment. Its leaden-grey and oily-brown plumage make a strikingly dark overall impression. The tail and wings are continually flicked on the ground. Its jerky, hopping movements are sparrow-like, but its build and needle-fine bill are more reminiscent of a warbler. From the top of a low bush the male delivers his pleasantly warbling song, rather like the wren's in tone but with a steadier rhythm. The call is a loud, distinct 'sih' or 'stieh'. Woods with dense undergrowth, thick hedges, conifer plantations and, often in the west, gardens and parks, are its haunts. Lives mainly on small seeds, but during the breeding season eats large numbers of insects.

Waxwing   *Bombycilla garrulus*   19 cm

Breeds in the coniferous forest of the Siberian Taiga, and in many years when food is scarce in autumn and winter is seen in flocks further south and west. In flight or perched looks like a starling from a distance. A distinctive, silvery trilling 'sirr' note, has a rising and falling ring when uttered by a flock on the wing. Lives on berries in winter and visits gardens and parks where there are rowan, cotoneaster, crab apple and dog-rose bushes retaining their fruit. Particularly in spring and summer also feeds on insects, neatly caught on the wing.

Wren

Dunnock

Waxwing

Wren

Dunnock

Waxwing

Warblers, flycatchers and thrushes
Family *Muscicapidae*

Most woodland perching birds belong to this enormous family. They find their food in different ways and the various groups make use of different woodland 'niches'. Warblers pick insects from the leaves of the trees and plants near the ground, flycatchers catch insects in flight and thrushes find food on the ground, in the soil and among dead leaves.

Warblers are small, fast moving, insectivorous and non-gregarious. The species are very much alike (within sub-families) and are best distinguished by their song. Because of their uniform plumage, constant movement in the shade among leaves and plants, and their similar calls, many, especially the willow warbler group, are sometimes indistinguishable in the field. Small points of detail such as leg colour and wing bars must be combined with posture and behaviour, haunt and song. Immatures resemble adults except in the case of the goldcrest. The warblers described here are divided into three genera: *Sylvia*, *Phylloscopus* and *Hippolais*.

Altogether 12 *Sylvia* species breed in Europe, six of them confined to the Mediterranean countries. In addition to those mentioned here, the Dartford warbler (*S. undata*) breeds in gorse bushes in southern England and western France.

Of the six *Phylloscopus* species breeding in Europe, the Arctic warbler (*P. borealis*) occurs in Arctic birch woods in the far north of Scandinavia and Bonelli's warbler (*P. bonelli*) in mountainous forests in central Europe and the Mediterranean countries. The goldcrest and firecrest (*Regulus*) are usually placed in this group.

Five species of *Hippolais* breed in Europe, two of them in the Mediterranean countries only and a third, *H. caligata*, only in European Russia.

Garden warbler

Fieldfare

Flycatchers are characterized by erect posture, flicking wings, scratchy calls and a habit of making sorties from strategic look-out points to catch flying insects. The bill base is broad, with long fine bristles. Juveniles are mottled. **Thrushes** are a heterogeneous group in size and appearance which can be divided into several sub-groups. The species described here are two redstart (*Phoenicurus*), the robin (*Erithacus*), two nightingale (*Luscinia*) and five thrush (*Turdus*). Altogether six *Turdus* species breed in Europe, but the ring ouzel (*T. torquatus*) breeds only in the mountains of western Scandinavia, the northern parts of the British Isles and in central Europe. Apart from these, two species of chat (*Saxicola*) breed in Europe north of the Mediterranean countries and Alps, the whinchat (*S. rubetra*) in open grasslands and the stonechat (*S. torquata*) on moorland and near the coast. The wheatear (*Oenanthe oenanthe*) breeds in open treeless country of various kinds, the red-flanked bluetail (*Tarsiger cyanurus*) breeds in coniferous forests in the extreme northeast of Europe and the bluethroat (*Luscinia svecica*) breeds in northerly wet bushy country. Many thrushes such as the robin and blackbird display surprising behavioural similarities. Both look for their food on the ground, hopping a few steps, standing motionless and listening with heads cocked on one side, rapidly seizing something edible and then hopping a few more steps. Sitting still and looking or listening for prey is a characteristic of all thrushes, which live mainly on insects, worms and snails, but will also take various tree fruits, especially in autumn and winter. Fruit and berries are the main winter diet of the true thrushes of the *Turdus* sub-family. The young, like those of the flycatchers, are speckled.

The various *Sylvia* species each inhabit special, but not easily definable, habitats within the various vegetation patterns of trees and bushes, ranging from the whitethroat in the hedges at the edge of a field to the blackcap in tall mature park woodland. Their songs consist partly of a '*Sylvia* waffle', i.e. a chattering, bubbling prattle, and partly of a rapid and often melodious flute solo. The harsh warning calls are also very similar. On the other hand, variations in plumage coloration between species are greater than in other warblers.

Blackcap *Sylvia atricapilla*   14 cm

Easily identified by its black or reddish brown cap. Although it shows itself more often than a garden warbler, usually only identified by the beautiful song from impenetrable foliage: a delightful bubbling melody, starting with an introductory squeak, turning into a fluting succession of softly articulated tones. The phrases are usually shorter than the garden warbler's, but include imitations of this and other species, and some chattering. The call is a 'teck', harsher and more energetic than the garden warbler's. There is also a 'cherr' and, when really perturbed, 'teck-teck-teck-teckcherrr'. Prefers mature, dense but airy deciduous woodland, but will breed in other habitats ranging from coniferous forest with occasional deciduous trees to parkland. Arrives in spring, much earlier than the garden warbler.

Barred warbler *Sylvia nisoria*   15 cm

From a distance looks dark grey with brown touches on its upper parts, and paler beneath. At closer quarters (although it is very shy) has crescentic markings and a 'hawk' eye. There are more differences than similarities between young barred warblers and garden warblers. The bold sandy grey has no olive green touches. The barred warbler, with long tail and thick beak, moves in an ungainly way, and when flying keeps a conspicuously straight and direct course about a metre above the ground. The male, perched on a bush or executing a wobbly, butterfly-like song flight over his territory, delivers a song resembling a slow version of the garden warbler's, but in tone like a sombre version of the blackcap's. Rough 'arr' sounds are mixed in with the song, and a rattling 'arrt-at-at-at' call. Prefers dry, sunlit, bushy ground with hawthorn, juniper and sloe. A rare but regular visitor to Britain, particularly the east coast, on migration.

Blackcap

Barred warbler

♂

♀

Blackcap

juvenile

♂

Barred warbler

Garden warbler *Sylvia borin* 14 cm

From a distance may seem to lack distinctive features with its uniformly warm brown suggesting a reed warbler. At close quarters, however, there are delicate shades on ochre flanks and mouse-grey sides to the throat, a gentle, round face and a distinct ring around the eye. Fresh plumage has pale-tipped wing feathers. Distinguished by its song, a babbling brook of clear notes and chattering but without the blackcap's fluting notes. The warning call is a 'tchack', often firmly and rhythmically repeated but softer and longer than the blackcap's, and also 'cherr'. Habitat choice same as the blackcap's, but is not dependent on trees and often chooses luxuriant undergrowth, venturing into dense but treeless scrub.

Lesser whitethroat *Sylvia curruca* 13.5 cm

An agile little songbird often only glimpsed in dense scrub or flying jerkily, tail hanging down, plunging like a dark shadow into a hedge. Dress varies in colour and shade, but short tail, dark legs, darker cheeks, a greyer, more uniform plumage and the absence of an eye ring make it different from the whitethroat. Its song is a short rattle on a single note and a '*Sylvia* waffle', often used as a pre-amble to the rattling note but also used separately as a sub-song, in which case it is hard to distinguish from the corresponding song of the whitethroat. Call is a resounding 'tchack' which becomes harsher and louder if disturbed.

Whitethroat *Sylvia communis* 14 cm

The male looks variegated for a warbler, while the female's colour is more uniform. The long white-edged tail, pale eyes and white eye ring, pale legs and chestnut edges of the secondaries distinguish both sexes from the lesser whitethroat. The song is scratchy, short and cheerful. Particularly at the start of the breeding season it also produces a continuous chatter more like the garden warbler's but interspersed with the typical call 'vedd, vedd, vedd'. When disturbed it will also emit a harsher, repetitive 'tcheck'. Frequents open sunlit places and the edges of woodland but never actually in a wood or forest.

Garden warbler

Lesser whitethroat

Whitethroat

Garden warbler

Lesser whitethroat

Whitethroat

♂

♀

Willow warbler *Phylloscopus trochilus* 11 cm

Very common. Distinguished from the chiffchaff by its song, a silvery descending trill, with an introduction like a delicate chaffinch. The call is a low 'whoo-eet', often slightly softer than the chiffchaff's. Plumage colour varies from one race to another, and with feather wear and tear, but is consistently paler than the chiffchaff, more yellow underneath, and with paler legs (although not always). Occurs in most types of open woodland and scrub with occasional deciduous trees.

Chiffchaff *Phylloscopus collybita* 11 cm

Distinguished from the willow warbler by its song, a jerky hiccough irregularly composed of 'chiff, chaff, chaff, chiff, chaff . . .' Summoning note, 'hweet', is similar to the willow warbler's but louder and monosyllabic. Drabber than the willow warbler, with dark, often greyish black legs. Frequents mature deciduous or mixed woodland, where the trees are too tall and close together for the willow warbler.

Greenish warbler *Phylloscopus trochiloides* 11 cm

Differs from the other *Phylloscopus* species by its song: like its movements and general character, it is fiery and impulsive. It often starts with a wagtail-like call 'tzli-vitt', continuing with a short, choppy sequence of similarly explosive high notes. Fresh plumage has a touch of greyish white, a pale narrow wing bar, yellow eye stripes and dark legs. When the plumage grows shabby the wing bars often vanish making it look like a willow warbler. Inhabits the edges of woodlands, and clumps of deciduous trees. Rare vagrant to Britain.

Wood warbler *Phylloscopus sibilatrix* 12.5 cm

Size, and bright, more distinct green and yellow plumage distinguish it from other *Phylloscopus* species. When seen from below it looks like an elongated triangle, with a pure white belly and a fairly wide bill base of a distinct orange shade. Song is a series of jingling 'zipp' sounds which accelerate and give way to a metallic trill. Its call, a plaintive 'tue', is typical and can be repeated as a song. Prefers airy deciduous woodland with tall old trees, especially beech woods.

Willow warbler   Chiffchaff   Greenish warbler   Wood warbler

juvenile

Willow warbler

Chiffchaff

Greenish warbler

Wood warbler

Melodious warbler *Hippolais polyglotta* 13 cm

Differs from the icterine by its song which is softer, faster and more chattery with
less repetition and without the long fiddle-scraping tones. The most characteristic
call, a house-sparrow-like chatter, is also woven into its song. An inconspicuous pale
wing panel (sometimes lacking) is the main plumage difference. Has a rounder head,
shorter wings, somewhat rounder and less colourful underparts and (usually)
browner legs. Haunts and behaviour resemble the icterine's but note the more
southerly distribution. Rare migrant to Britain.

Icterine warbler *Hippolais icterina* 13.5 cm

A little larger than melodious warbler, but its more domed head (breeding season
only) and upright posture make it look quite hefty. The two are hard to distinguish
except by song. In fresh plumage, however, the icterine has a pale wing panel and grey
legs. The powerful song, which includes repetition and mimicry, is characterized by
high, shrill notes. The typical call, a soft but explosive 'hippolyit', is sometimes also
woven in. Also has a repeated resonant 'tack' like the blackcap's. Breeds in open
deciduous or mixed woods. Distribution more northerly than that of melodious
warbler, and a rare migrant in Britain.

Goldcrest *Regulus regulus* 9 cm

Small and attractive. Reveals its presence by soft high-pitched squeaks – 'zii-zii-
zii ... zii ... zi', thinner than the calls of the coal tit. The song is at the same high
pitch, a delicately descending 'zih sissisiu-sih sissisiu-sih, sissisietuit' (see treecreeper,
p. 102). The young do not have stripes on the head. Prefers coniferous or mixed
woodland with spruce trees. Lives on small insects and their larvae. Often gathers
in small groups in autumn and is a typical ingredient of migrating tit or warbler
flocks (see p. 96).

Firecrest *Regulus ignicapillus* 9 cm

Distinguished from the very similar goldcrest by broad white eyestripes and dark
markings around its eyes. Song less complicated and gains in volume towards the
end, 'sissisisisisitt'. Call 'peep' is distinguishable from the goldcrest's. Usually seen
in deciduous woodland on the continent but the small British breeding population
is restricted to conifers.

Melodious warbler	Icterine warbler	Goldcrest	Firecrest

Melodious warbler

Icterine warbler

juvenile

♀ Goldcrest ♂

juvenile

♀ ♂ Firecrest

Spotted flycatcher   *Muscicapa striata*   14 cm

An odd man out among the perching birds. Its long-winged flycatcher manner and inconspicuous markings make it easily recognizable. At a distance, in silhouette, the head shape alone makes it different from other flycatchers. Moves gently in the air with sweeping motions and rather slow, barely perceptible wing beats. Often hovers fluttering, and sideslips adroitly. A mid-air snap is audible when the stout mandibles close on its main diet, flying insects. Emits a soft, scrapy 'ptsirr' or 'tsii' from its perch. Its very limited song is a few quasi-call prolonged scrapings drawn to and fro three or four times. The young have pale mottling on the upper parts. Widespread, although not in dense woodland, it generally prefers sunny, open ground with occasional trees, and is often found in village gardens. Nests under eaves, in holes in walls, in nestboxes and on broken tree trunks. Winters in southern Africa, and is one of the latest summer visitors to arrive back in Europe.

Red-breasted flycatcher   *Ficedula parva*   11.5 cm

Black and white tail markings distinguish it from other flycatchers and other small grey-brown perching birds. Always looks small, with an alert posture and eager movements. Its eyes look big and the broad bill base often has a yellow shine in back lighting. The male's red bib does not develop until he is two or possibly three years old. Hard to spot in its natural surroundings, because it prefers to keep in the crowns of the trees, where it is constantly on the move. Its easily missed song is similar in form and tone to those of several species nesting in the same surroundings. Most often it appears to be divided into two sections; an introduction which may resemble wood warbler or tree pipit, and a second half performed in the willow warbler's style. Broadly, it resembles the pied flycatcher, but the tone is lighter and the key more melancholy; it is liable to be confused with the willow warbler's. Its wren-like chattering is perhaps more distinctive. Lives on insects caught in the air and picked off branches and leaves inside the canopy and not in the open air like the spotted flycatcher. Breeds mostly in tall deciduous and mixed woods, rarely in conifers. Only occasional stray migrants occur in western Europe.

Spotted flycatcher

Red-breasted flycatcher

Spotted flycatcher

♂

juvenile

Red-breasted flycatcher

♀

Pied flycatcher

Collared flycatcher

juvenile

Pied flycatcher *Ficedula hypoleuca* 13 cm

Posture and manner are instantly revealing. Has a distinctive habit of flapping its wings. The males' upper parts vary from sooty black to greyish brown, and these greyish brown 'female-coloured' males predominate in eastern central Europe. They are distinguishable from the females by the white forehead patch. After moulting in July and August, both sexes and all ages are white below and greyish brown above, which make them indistinguishable in the field. Females cannot be reliably distinguished from collared flycatcher females. Pied flycatcher song varies a great deal and can be confused with the redstart's, but is less melodious. Also emits a short 'pwitt' and a harsh 'pick' or, when annoyed, a rapidly repeated 'pick, pick, pick ...' Breeds in coniferous but more often in old deciduous woods and builds its nest in holes. It likes nestboxes, and one male may maintain two females and their broods in neighbouring boxes. Lives on insects caught in the air.

Collared flycatcher *Ficedula albicollis* 12.5 cm

Male easily distinguished from a pied by the white collar and rump. Females of the two species are almost alike. The collared makes itself known by its characteristic call, a full-throated 'ihp' or 'hiep', similar to the warning note of the nightingale. Its song is a slow rubbing and squeaking noise, often rounded off with a grumpy finish. Sometimes a number of bright 'zitly, zitly, zitly ...' sounds are woven in. Nests in nestboxes and hollow trees in mature deciduous woods. Diet and behaviour resemble the pied's but it usually perches higher in the trees. An eastern species, very rare on migration in Britain.

♀

Pied flycatcher

♂

♀

♂

Collared flycatcher

Redstart *Phoenicurus phoenicurus*   14 cm

The brick-red tail is the most striking characteristic. Despite his beautiful plumage, the male often remains unnoticed until he takes to the air and shows his tail. Has a bold, erect posture when perching, and at regular intervals sets his tail quivering slightly. Females differ from black redstart females and young males by their pale, usually white throat and much paler underparts. Like the flycatchers, redstarts often perch on the look-out, but usually dive to the ground after prey. One of the first woodland perching birds to wake up, the male's song is at its height about dawn. Its scratchy song, which resembles the pied flycatcher or a robin, often mimics other birds and nearly always starts with a 'hyitt' and then a rolling 'tui-tui-tui-tui'. The call, like the willow warbler's, is often combined with the alarm note to form a 'huit-chuuck-chuuck', a characteristic of the species. Breeds in open woodland and parkland, nesting in natural cavities or nestboxes. Lives on insects and their larvae.

Black redstart *Phoenicurus ochruros*   14 cm

When the male's colours are fully developed he is easily recognized by his sooty plumage and white wing patch. The female resembles a grimy female redstart but always has a darker chin and belly. The male, until he acquires full plumage when he is two years old, resembles a darker edition of the female. In much of Europe breeds in towns and villages, which have replaced the original rocky mountain environment. The male sings from chimneys, television aerials or church towers. The song is often 'amplified' as it echoes between streets and concrete façades, making the bird astonishingly hard to trace. The song is more or less divided into three or four strenuously uttered phrases. These vary, but often there is a sharp introductory 'svi-svi-svi-svi-svi' something like the wren, together with a distinctive gravel-like crunching. The call is terser than the redstart's; a 'tsip' or, when the bird is annoyed, 'tsip-tsip-tsip', often accompanied by 'tack-tack-tack'. Similar diet to the redstart's, but more often catches insects on the wing. Sometimes hovers alongside walls and under eaves.

Redstart

Black redstart

♂ autumn

♀

Redstart

♂

♀

Black redstart

♂

Robin *Erithacus rubecula* 14 cm

The robin's olive-brown tail distinguishes it from the rufous tail of the nightingale. The robin also has an unmistakable song; a cascade or burst of crystal clear notes, racing past, dying away and then blazing into a new outburst. A more fragile version brightens sunny winter days. It also has a gently snapping 'tick' and a slow sighing 'sih'. On the continent, the robin is unobtrusive and in the north is mostly seen in dense spruce woods. Further south and west its habitat choice is more catholic, and in the British Isles it commonly nests in gardens and can be very tame. Lives on various ground invertebrates and in autumn and winter also eats fruit and berries.

Thrush nightingale *Luscinia luscinia* 16.5 cm

It is difficult to distinguish between the two nightingale species in the field solely by plumage. The thrush is darker, more of an olive-brown, and its breast and flanks are mottled. Immature plumage resembles the robin's, but the tail is rufous. A very withdrawn bird, its favourite haunt is on the ground among low, dense, damp thickets, where it often keeps within a very limited area. Its song can be heard quite far away and includes bright, energetic whistlings, hollow, muffled flute tones and atonal rattlings. Most thrush nightingales have a slower, more accented and monotonous song than the nightingale with regularly repeated phrases. The call is a short, sharp 'tsitt'. Feeds on insects, worms and snails and, in autumn, on berries and fruit. A scarce vagrant to Britain.

Nightingale *Luscinia megarhynchos* 16.5 cm

The southern and western counterpart of the thrush nightingale. More uniformly coloured than the latter, with faintly reddish-brown upper parts and light grey flanks. In habits and haunts resembles the thrush nightingale but prefers drier areas of scrub and deciduous woodland. Its song resembles that of the other species, except that it includes a sequence in which a reiterated fluting 'piu' rises to a crescendo. Although there is individual variation, the song performances of the nightingale are generally somewhat more passionate than those of the thrush nightingale and sometimes include phrases resembling those produced by *Acrocephalus* warblers. Its other calls resemble those of the thrush nightingale, but it often also produces a 'hui' and 'chack'.

Robin

Thrush nightingale

Nightingale

Robin

juvenile

Thrush nightingale

Nightingale

Fieldfare

Mistle thrush

Blackbird *Turdus merula* 25 cm

One of the commonest birds in the countryside and gardens. Young in their first plumage are dark brown with rufous stripes. Seen on the ground more often than other thrushes, and when frightened often retreats under a hedge or bush, protesting with a series of clucking 'tchack' sounds which gradually turn into a shrill metallic screeching. It is an excellent and alert watchdog of impending danger, such as cats. From inside bushes or secluded corners or as it crosses a lawn or drive, it announces its presence with a searing high pitched 'srrii'. Perhaps best known for its song, heard as early as February. From television aerials, chimneys or tree tops males produce a song which alternates between flute-like tones and yodelling or twittering. Breeds in luxuriant woodland undergrowth, as well as around our homes. Lives on worms, insects, fruits and berries.

Fieldfare *Turdus pilaris* 25.5 cm

A regular and numerous winter visitor to western Europe, particularly Britain. The rufous back, grey rump and black tail present a striking contrast. Like the mistle thrush, the white triangle on the wing underside is a conspicuous flight feature. Like magpie croakings, the fieldfare's notes are difficult to describe yet highly characteristic: usually a chuckling 'chack-chack-chack (-chackarr)' in action, and a delicate 'sii' on the wing. Its song is a completely unmusical squeaking interspersed with chattering. Often associates with other thrushes in fields of short grass to use their typical technique of listening for worms and then pulling them from the ground. Diet also includes other small soil invertebrates, fruit and berries. Nests in northeast Europe in woods of tall birch or pine trees.

Blackbird

Fieldfare

Blackbird

♂

♀

Fieldfare

Redwing *Turdus iliacus* 21 cm

Red flanks and underwings, and heavy facial markings are the most important characteristics. Distinguished from the song thrush by its flight call, a delicately sliding 'tsuiip'. In the autumn young birds have a rust-yellow wash over head and breast. The song is in two parts: a few loud fluting tones and then a low, almost continuous, agitated twittering. The fluting tones vary, but because the birds imitate each other there is usually only one variety within an area. Also emits a subdued 'koek' and a loud rattling warning note. Breeds in lower and bushier country than the fieldfare. Now breeding in northern Britain, but widespread and numerous in winter. Feeds on soil invertebrates in summer and winter fruit in autumn.

Song thrush *Turdus philomelos* 23 cm

Much smaller than the mistle. In flight resembles a redwing but is distinguished by its short ticking flight call, 'zip', and pale yellowish underwings. The song is a soft flute-like tone of curt phrases, each repeated three or four times and then followed by the next after a brief pause. Mimicry is frequent. This bird has adjusted to the differing ecological conditions between western and continental Europe and northern and eastern Europe. In the north it is shy, breeding in damp, mossy coniferous and mixed woodland with abundant ground vegetation; while in the British Isles it is also common in parks and gardens. Lives on worms, snails, insects and, in autumn, various fruits and berries.

Mistle thrush *Turdus viscivorus* 27 cm

An undulating flight, a dove-like way of retracting its wings and an olive-fawn rump. In the mixed flocks of thrushes in the autumn, can be confused with fieldfares, but is distinguished by the lack of contrast between tail and rump and by the white tips of its outer tail feathers, visible when it lands (see p. 92). In most cases, however, can be recognized by its flight note, a dry rattling 'rrrr'. Often in song before winter has ended, sounds like a poorly developed blackbird singing on a lonely mountain. It consists of short, flute-like phrases with long pauses in between. Breeds early, in open mature woodland; in western Europe it also nests in large gardens and parks. Lives on worms, soil invertebrates, fruits and berries.

Redwing

Song thrush

Mistle thrush

Redwing

Song thrush

Mistle thrush

Tits *Paridae*

Small lively birds feeding mostly on insects, seeds and fruit. Most species are sedentary in Europe, but when food is in short supply (particularly in the east) they can migrate for considerable distances (great, blue, coal tit). During the winter season several tit species often wander around in small flocks, usually keeping within a limited area. They are often joined by gold-crests, treecreepers, wrens, nuthatches and the odd small woodpecker. Tits usually move rapidly and acrobatically among the branches, keeping in touch by their contact calls. Several species will 'cache' food stores for winter and then each species will keep to a certain part of each tree, ensuring efficient exploitation of the available food, and that none go hungry. This apportionment is very noticeable in the north among willow, crested and coal tits, which live only in coniferous areas. In general, willow tits keep close to the trunk, crested tits to the middle portions of the branches and coal tits furthest out on the uppermost branches. Further south, great tits feed on or near the ground, blue tits in the canopy and long-tailed tits at the extreme ends of the twigs.

Long-tailed tit   *Aegithalos caudatus*   14 cm

A tiny fluffy ball of wool with a tail longer than its body. The northern race has an all-white head, but elsewhere the head has black stripes. In mixed flocks, the long-tailed is immediately identifiable by its frequent and intensively squeaking summoning note, a short buzzing 'tserr' interspersed with a clicking 'teck'. In autumn and winter these birds form small close-knit family groups. Before flying over open country they gather to the accompaniment of eager, piercing trisyllabic 'tsi-tsi-tsis' and then cross over in Indian file, eagerly calling all the way. The song, seldom heard, is a fine trill like the blue tit's. Catholic in habitat, frequenting open woodland, scrub, and farmland with bushes and hedges. Lives mainly on small insects and spiders. Its nest, cunningly built of feathers, moss and cobwebs, is flask-shaped and entered through a hole in the side. Young birds in the family party, not themselves ready to breed, will assist the parent birds to feed the nestlings.

Long-tailed tit

Long-tailed tit

northern and eastern race

continental race

Blue tit *Parus caeruleus*

11.5 cm

Calls are very variable. Its beautifully clear silver song is a frequent, persistently ringing 'psi-tsi-sirrrrrrrr'. Also often produces a shrill, rather cheeky 'cherrecherre-cherre', a bouncing 'ptsi-tsi-di-di-di', a 'pizitzeh' and a soft 'ptsi'. It prefers to breed in holes in open deciduous or mixed woodland and is a frequent inhabitant of garden nestboxes. In autumn and winter, woodland birds commonly move into reedbeds or gardens, searching for wintering insects, larvae and chrysalids. Primarily an insectivore, eats fewer seeds and fruit than the great tit.

Great tit *Parus major*

14 cm

Despite striking plumage the great tit causes recognition problems because of its many and varied calls. In all these calls one can discern a special, typical, timbre, although deception by some atypical sound is not uncommon. Its song is usually a pleasantly monotonous combination of a bi-syllabic 'tee-chaah tee-chaah ...' The female has a much thinner breast stripe than the male and fledglings have a brownish crown and yellowish cheeks. In the picture opposite, showing two males, the bird on the right is displaying the bright markings of his underparts in what is termed a threat posture. The great tit breeds in holes in all kinds of woodland, rearing one brood in deciduous woods and two in conifers. Much of its food is seeds and fruit, but especially during the breeding season it feeds on insects, larvae and other invertebrates.

Coal tit *Parus ater*

11.5 cm

Distinguished from the great tit by its extended white nape, the lack of a stripe on the breast, its size and browner coloration. It also has a proportionately larger head. Its quick and restless movements are more similar to the goldcrest's. It prefers conifers and is often seen with goldcrests. When looking for food it emits a thin 'psit' or 'ppsittsitsi'. Other common calls are a clear flute-like 'puht', a bright 'piht' and a goldcrest-like 'si-si-si'. The song variants can be likened to a diminutive great tit, though simpler, speeded up, and brighter in tone. It also has a very high and crystal clear tremolo. Nests in holes in trees, walls or the ground. Primarily a bird of coniferous woodland, feeding on insects and seeds. Regularly visits other habitats (including garden bird tables) in autumn and winter. Shortage of food can provoke invasion-like emigrations from eastern Europe, bringing the brighter-plumaged continental race west to Britain.

Blue tit

Great tit

Coal tit

Blue tit

Great tit

Coal tit

Marsh tit *Parus palustris*   11.5 cm

Lacks the willow tit's pale wing panel, has a shorter bib, and gives the impression of a smaller head, slimmer neck, and a shinier black cap. Young birds, however, have a duller cap and adults in fresh plumage can have the suggestion of a pale wing panel. The two species are most easily distinguished by their calls. The marsh tit has an explosive 'pitschu' and a repetitive 'tscheu-tscheu-tscheu', often combined to form 'psitittcheh-cheh-cheh-cheh'. Song includes a series of monotonously repeated notes – 'tchip-tchip …' Frequents deciduous or mixed woodlands often close to small rivers and lakesides, nesting in holes close to the ground, and will occasionally visit gardens. Lives on insects and seeds from shrubs and grasses.

Willow tit *Parus montanus*   11.5 cm

The pale wing panel, large head and fluffier plumage distinguish willow from marsh tits. In the southern race (*montanus*) the rust-coloured flanks, and the white cheeks of the Scandinavian race (*borealis*) are distinguishing characteristics. The most typical note is a long, rough, nasal 'teh-teh-teh'. Tits keep in touch with each other by a short squeaky 'ti-ti'. Their song is a repetitive 'tu-tu-tu-tu-tu', like the wood warbler's, or a buzzing 'zi-zezerrr'. In Scandinavia the willow tit is seen in coniferous and mixed woodland, while the southern race prefers damp deciduous woodland. Lives on insects, seeds and berries. Unlike other tits, it excavates its nest hole in rotten wood – hence the powerful neck muscles that give the 'bull-necked' appearance.

Crested tit *Parus cristatus*   11.5 cm

Like many of the tit species, first attracts notice by its note. When it is clearly visible, its uniformly dull greyish-brown upper parts are very often its most striking feature, then the head markings so typical of the species. Its call is a rolling or ringing 'prililill' or a delicate 'tsii'. Its song, which has the same ringing character as the call, oscillates between two pitches, 'prililill-prelelell-prililill …'. A typical inhabitant of coniferous woodlands, seldom seen outside continuous woodland or forest. Feeds on spiders, insects and seeds, especially spruce. Lays up food for the winter.

Marsh tit

Willow tit

Crested tit

Marsh tit

Willow tit

Scandinavian

Crested tit

Nuthatch *Sitta europaea* 14 cm

Perky, saucy-looking and always on the move on tree trunks and branches. Underparts range from the uniform reddish brown of the western and southern races to the pale belly of Scandinavian nuthatches (*europaea*), in which only the flanks are brown shaded. The rufous-chestnut of the flanks and 'armpit' of the male is richer than the female. The nuthatch's calls advertise its presence in thick-trunked oak trees. Sings with a piercing 'piu, piu, piu ...' and a clear 'vivivivivivi ...' Also produces clear notes such as 'huit' and 'chut', a nasal 'qut' and a sharp 'sitt, sitt, sitt'. Young birds beg for food from the nesting hole with a delicate 'srii, srii ...' Found in deciduous woods and parks, preferring groups of old oak trees. Lives on spiders, insects, nuts and seeds and occasionally eggs or nestlings. Visits bird tables regularly. Has the unusual habit of putting mud walling around its nest hole if the opening is too large.

Short-toed treecreeper *Certhia brachydactyla* 12.5 cm

Differs from the treecreeper by its call, because its rust-coloured flanks and fractionally longer bill are usually impossible to observe. Different areas of distribution, and on the continent the preference of the short-toed species for deciduous trees, are other distinctive points. Shorter song than the treecreeper's, far more penetrating, fiercely and jerkily performed, 'sitt, sitt, sitteroitt'. Also has a piercing high 'zrrieh' and a clear 'zut'. Frequents thick-trunked trees in deciduous woods, parks and avenues, and pine trees in Mediterranean countries.

Treecreeper *Certhia familiaris* 12.5 cm

Hard to tell from the short-toed treecreeper except by its call. A frail, neat-looking bird, it climbs in a jerky spiral up tree trunks always head uppermost. After inspecting a crowded section of one trunk it will abruptly descend, wings fluttering, to the bottom of the next tree and climb again. May advertise itself with a piercing high-pitched 'zrriht' or 'zieet'. Song has the tone of the wren's and comprises many repetitive notes, rounded off with a fine trill. Often wanders with tit flocks. Found in woods and parks with scattered conifers, and lives on insects and spiders. In Britain, where it is the only treecreeper, it occurs in all types of woodland.

Nuthatch

Short-toed treecreeper

Treecreeper

northern race

Short-toed
treecreeper

Nuthatch

Treecreeper

Sparrows *Ploceidae*

An adjunct to the African and Asian weaver family, represented in Europe by five species. The two included here are more or less associated with human habitation. They live mainly on seeds, preferably picked up from the ground, and on insects. They are gregarious, and the house sparrow often breeds in colonies.

Finches *Fringillidae*

All finches have a relatively thick bill, live more or less permanently in flocks and have an undulating flight. They can be mainly recognized by call, bill shape, wing markings and rump colour. The song of the chaffinch, brambling and rosefinch is simple, very audible and very typical, while the song of other species has more individual variation and complexity. Some species sing during a so-called 'butterfly' flight, the male slowly flying over his territory with deep and distinct wing beats. The young are mainly reared on seeds, but in the first few days of life insects may be the major food. The differently shaped beaks of the various species are adapted to groups of seeds or berries, which reduces competition between those living in the same area. The degree of specialization varies a good deal, however; the chaffinch has a very wide-ranging diet, while crossbills are more limited to a particular kind of food. In winter finches rove in flocks, gathering where food is abundant. Many of the species visit places where food is put out for them.

Buntings *Emberizidae*

A group of perching birds mainly attached to cultivated areas, scrub and marshlands. They bear some resemblances to finches but have a relatively long tail, tufted crown and like to spend much time on the ground. Their beaks are adapted for a diet of seeds, but the young are fed on insects. Of the 13 species occurring in Europe, there are three (north of the Mediterranean countries and Alps) which occur in semi-open bushy ground and gardens. The yellowhammer (*Emberiza citrinella*) breeds commonly in scrub and hedges close to open areas. It visits places where food is put out. It can be recognized by its rust-coloured rump. The cirl bunting (*E. cirlus*) occurs in farmland (from southern England, France and further south) and the ortolan bunting (*E. hortulana*) in bushy, often waterlogged semi-open ground over large parts of Europe excluding the British Isles.

first winter ♂ ♀ Yellowhammer

Tree sparrow   *Passer montanus*   14 cm

Easily distinguished from the house sparrow by its completely red-brown crown, black cheek spots and conspicuous white collar. The sexes are identical in appearance. Like the house sparrow, it nests near towns and villages, but is not as urbanized. Also occurs in open farmland where it may build in nestboxes or cavities in clumps of trees or on the edges of woods. More mobile than the house sparrow and sometimes accompanies other finches and *Emberizidae* to feed in the fields. The flock often flies past at considerable speed in close formation, making a bee-line for its target, and the birds are identified by their harsh call, a rapidly repeated 'teck, teck, teck ...' They often keep company inside hedges and bushes with house sparrows, chattering with a house-sparrow-like 'trettrett'. The tree sparrow is a seed eater, but its diet also includes insects. Often occupies nestboxes intended for redstarts, flycatchers and other birds, even displacing the original occupants. One way of preventing this is to put the nestboxes about 1.5 or 2 metres off the ground, because these birds seldom nest below that height.

House sparrow   *Passer domesticus*   15–18 cm

Mainly a town and city bird, and the chirruping flocks in park hedges or garden bushes are unmistakable. Could be confused with the tree sparrow, but it has a reddish brown crown, black cheeks and a more yellowish brown rump. The house sparrow may be less easy to identify in farming country, especially the female, whose dress is strikingly uninteresting. The male is more resplendent in fully developed plumage, but in smoky cities his feathers often become grimy, and then the plumage looks very dark. When the birds moult, between August and October, males acquire a more brown-fawn dress in which the black bib is obscured by pale feather edges and the grey and liver-brown parts of the head almost turn to a fawn colour. These pale fringes gradually wear away and the birds are at their brightest in early summer. Their note is a chatter with monotonous 'chip', 'chap' or 'chirp' sounds, quite deafening when taken up by a large flock. In flight they also emit a shorter 'tvit'. Eats almost anything, but seeds and insects are its basic diet, and it can be a pest on cereal crops. Nests in cavities of various kinds, most often under roof tiles, but can nest openly in a tree or bush, where the nest will be large, skilfully constructed, domed and provided with a side entrance, reminiscent of a weaver's nest in Africa. These large nests in the open are fairly common in southern Europe.

Tree sparrow

House sparrow

Tree sparrow

♀

House sparrow   ♂ display

♂

Chaffinch *Fringilla coelebs* 15.5 cm

The male is easily recognized, but the female is more neutral in appearance. White leading edges to the wings, white wing bars and white outer tail feathers are easily observable characteristics in both sexes whether perching or in flight. After its autumn moult the male acquires feathers with fringes of brown-beige, so that its head in particular is very similar to the female's. However, these edges are gradually worn away before the breeding season. The song is an accelerating verse with an abrupt cadenza. It varies from one area to another but is always resonant and clearly audible, and is used by the male to announce that a particular area is occupied. The chaffinch's territory, like the brambling's, is relatively large, and all breeding activities are conducted within its boundaries. Its summoning note is a loud, resonant 'fink', its flight note is a softer 'yupp' and its warning note a monotonously repeated 'hwitt'. A common breeding bird in woods, parks, gardens or around copses or tall hedges in farming country. In winter chaffinches spend a great deal of time in farming country, often with other finches. These flocks are often predominantly, or entirely, of one sex. During the breeding season it lives to a large extent on insects, but otherwise it lives on seeds.

Brambling *Fringilla montifringilla* 15.5 cm

Takes the place of the chaffinch in northern Europe, breeding in birch woods and willow scrub in the taiga, where it is very common. At a distance it is most easily recognized by its brilliant white rump, although some young females lack this feature. At closer quarters it has a mottled appearance, with orange breast and shoulders. The male has more distinct markings than the female, and in winter he has a very bright yellow bill with a dark tip. Towards late winter and spring, the male bird's head and the darker portion of his mantle become coal black as the pale feather-tips are worn away. In flight bramblings constantly communicate with a typical monotonous croaking 'esh' or 'chway'. The song, sometimes performed by the male when soaring, is a prolonged bleating 'dshweeeh' like the greenfinch's. Migrates south and west in winter, and flocks (often with chaffinches) will then congregate around fields and woodland areas. Beechmast and hornbeam seeds are its favourite food, and flocks of bramblings will often gather in beech woods where there is plenty of mast.

Chaffinch

Brambling

Chaffinch

♂

♀

♂ winter

Brambling
winter

♀

♂

Siskin *Carduelis spinus*   12.5 cm

The perching male's contrasting yellow, green and black plumage is easy to recognize. Females are a washier grey but differ from the redpoll by touches of green and yellow. Lives on seeds extracted from half-open conifer scales with its pointed bill. Thus its breeding in an area depends on the availability of spruce seeds. Only seen very occasionally for short periods in spring and summer, and is mostly revealed by its song. The male trills forth a rolling song with alternating pitches, often ending with a protracting rasping 'krriee'. When the fledglings have learned to fly and the cone seeds fall in late summer, siskin flocks move into the surrounding country. Alder and birch seeds are then their principal diet, and the energetic birds can be seen elegantly suspended, often upside down, like tits, from the branches. They fly from one tree to another in bobbing, unsteady trajectory, with rough calls and loud 'siluh' or 'tseew' sounds. Now a regular garden visitor to feed on peanuts.

Greenfinch *Chloris chloris*   15 cm

Largest of the yellow-green finches, of 'muscular' build and with a stout bill. In autumn its basic colour is an inconspicuous, drab olive-green, but it has a yellow strip along the wing (and, sometimes, a yellow-green belly). The tail markings are not really noticeable unless the bird is seen in flight or displaying aggressively at a bird table. These tail markings make a brilliant show when a group flies up from a roadside or a garden path where there are wild plants with plenty of seeds. In flight it produces a quick, bouncy 'chirirrip', and its call is a soft 'soo-eet'. As the breeding season approaches, the male advertises his presence from a lofty song perch with a prolonged sizzling, bleating 'dzweeh' and a series of rolling whistlings and twitterings. During the most intensive period the male also stages a song flight on slow-moving wings. By this time (from March onwards) wear and tear on his dress has brought out the bright yellow-green more clearly. Two-year-old males can be a magnificent canary-yellow beneath, with smart grey wings and a golden-olive mantle. Common in open, treed country, ranging from city parks and gardens to farmland with substantial hedges or scrub, and woodland clearings. Lives on seeds in winter and visits bird tables if hemp, sunflower seeds or peanuts are put out.

Siskin

Greenfinch

♀

♂

juvenile

Siskin

juvenile

♂

Greenfinch

♀

Goldfinch *Carduelis carduelis* 13 cm

Approach heralded with a typically soft but rather sharp 'stickelitt'. Whether flying in deep undulations or adorning the tops of burdocks, thistles or teazels, their many colours are outstanding. The young differ from those of the siskin and greenfinch by their completely black tail and typical wing markings, which resemble those of the adult birds. They may have fawn 'juvenile' heads until mid-October, and then they moult and resemble adults. The male's song is a typically finch-like silvery tinkling, with interwoven flight calls. Relatively short tarsi and long pointed bill allow it to extract the deeply concealed seeds of prickly plants such as thistle and burdock. In autumn and winter wandering flocks can be seen on areas of rough ground and woodland clearings where winter plants flourish. The young in their first few days are mostly reared on insects. During spring and summer the goldfinch breeds in copses, thick hedges, open broadleaved woods and gardens, constructing a typically finch-like, neat nest of moss, lichens and fine rootlets lined with hair.

Bullfinch *Pyrrhula pyrrhula* 16 cm

Both sexes easily recognized by their black bonnet, white wing bars and white rump. Young birds resemble females but lack the black bonnet, and their wing bars are dirty white. The birds in the British Isles are slightly smaller and duller in colour than their continental cousins. The very rarely heard song is a subdued staccato chattering with creaking notes and interwoven soft whistlings. The call is a soft plaintive whistling 'jooh'. Leads a secluded life in dense scrub or woodland, and it is usually this note which reveals his presence. During late autumn and winter the males' red bellies are obvious when a group is quietly working through the fruit on an ash or rowan tree. In winter and spring, when other food is hard to come by, it readily visits gardens, orchards (where it may reach pest status on pears) and similar places for the soft tree buds which form part of its diet. Also eats fresh berries and large soft-skinned seeds from shrubs. Its blunt parrot-like beak is adapted to this diet. It prefers taking its food direct from branches and stalks and seldom picks food from the ground. Breeds in broadleaved woods and overgrown gardens. The nest, a flat platform of fine twigs with a shallow cup, resembles a miniature woodpigeon's nest.

Goldfinch

Bullfinch

Goldfinch

juvenile

juvenile

♂

♀

Bullfinch

Hawfinch *Coccothraustes coccothraustes* 18 cm

Despite its brilliant markings and formidable beak, the hawfinch is frequently over-looked. It is shy and retiring and mainly advertises its presence with an explosive 'zick' or a hissing 'srri'. When sighted it is a fat, squat finch, usually passing through a forest clearing at tree top height, in an undulating flight with the white wing bars its most conspicuous feature, or suddenly taking off from a wooded slope, in which case its white tail marking will also clearly stand out. In both adults and young the beak is blue-grey in summer and yellowish in winter. Young birds have fawn-coloured breasts and less conspicuous face and throat markings. The female is duller with less contrasting plumage than the male. Occurs sparsely in broadleaved and mixed woods and in orchard country. Its oversize beak can exert a pressure of 14 kilograms per square centimetre, and is ideal for breaking hard stones such as cherries or sloes to reach the nutritious kernel. It often searches on the ground beneath fruit trees for stones of fallen fruit, but lives mainly on beech mast, mountain ash, hornbeam and elm seeds, as well as buds and insects.

Serin *Serinus serinus* 11.5 cm

Often appears in pairs or small groups, in which the male is easily recognized by his canary-yellow markings. When taking to the wing its yellow rump, dark tail and absence of bright wing markings are good recognition features. Other striking features are its small size and short stubby beak. Serins are often hard to spot so their note is very useful for recognition purposes. In flight it is usually a tinkling 'tirrillillit' or 'zr'r'rillitt', but they also have a less readily identified 'dyui' like the greenfinch. A very distinctive song – persistent and rapid like splintered glass – can be heard from a tree top or during a high circling song flight. Occurs in parks, gardens and farming country with scattered clumps of trees, preferably with the odd conifer, while in the Mediterranean countries it is most often found in thin pine woods. Lives on the seeds of various trees, grass and shrubs, often picking them off the ground, hence the short blunt beak.

Hawfinch

Serin

Hawfinch

♀

♂

Serin

♂

♀

Redpoll   *Acanthis flammea*   13–15 cm

The several races vary widely in colour and size. The British and central European race (*cabaret*), which also occasionally breeds in Denmark, is smaller and darker than the northern Scandinavian (*flammea*) which occasionally overwinters in Britain. Young birds lack the black and red facial markings of adults. Fluffy plumage and the male bird's breeding season pink rump and breast are also striking. The flock's movements between birches or alders are like those of the siskins but the flight call, an eagerly reiterated 'dyeck, dyeck, dyeck', differs from its rougher notes. The call is a soft, slightly querying 'dyuii'. The occurrences of redpolls outside their breeding areas are extremely variable; in some years they seem to be everywhere but in others very scarce. The purring display song is produced in a circling flight high above the trees.

Linnet   *Acanthis cannabina*   13.5 cm

Older males are magnificently dressed in summer and cannot be confused with other finches. In flight they show a brown back and whitish wing patches. Females can be harder to identify, but the birds usually appear in pairs or flocks, making recognition less difficult. Typical cheek markings give the bird a distinctive facial expression. The flight call, reminiscent of the greenfinch's, is an unevenly reverberating 'tett-tett-terrett'. Performed full scale from a bush top the song is very beautiful – ingeniously interwoven twitterings, trills and flute-like tones. Sometimes, however, both sexes produce what is almost small-talk, with delicate tinklings and cheerful twitters. Mainly inhabits gardens, scrub, woodland clearings and farmland, breeding in bushes but overwintering more commonly on weedy ground and stubble fields.

The twite (*A. flavirostris*), a close relative of the linnet, winters along the coasts of western Europe and the southern Baltic. Differs from the linnet by its uniform honey-yellow coloration, yellow beak in winter and male's pink rump.

Redpoll
Linnet

Rosefinch or
scarlet grosbeak
Crossbill
Parrot crossbill
Descriptions on p. 118

continental
and
British race

Scandinavian race

Redpoll

♂

♂ autumn

Linnet

♀

Rosefinch (scarlet grosbeak) *Carpodacus erythrinus*

14.5 cm

Distinguished from other reddish finches by the combination of bright red head, throat and rump, which the male does not acquire until his second year. The brightness and extent of the red often varies. Unlike many other finches, often occurs singly, when young males and females can be hard to identify. Look for the fairly stout bullfinch-like bill and drab plumage brightened only by the double wing bars. The flight is undulating and the call a soft 'dyui', sometimes clear but usually a hoarse bleat. The male, who arrives in northern and eastern Europe as late as the end of May, sings a catchy but rather despondent 'ste-vidye-vidyue'. Breeds where there are plenty of bushes and lives on seeds, buds, berries and insects. The species is rapidly spreading westward, and occurs regularly in western Europe as a migrant. Unfortunately, the species is often kept in captivity, but frequently escapes, surviving well in the wild.

Crossbill *Loxia curvirostra*

17 cm

Big and stocky, of squat proportions. Look for the male's red rump and the female's greenish yellow rump in flight. The pale fawn double wing bars of young birds can confuse them with the young of the Siberian two-barred crossbill (*L. leucopteria*), although this occasional visitor to the west has wider and white wing bars and distinct white scapular tips. One- and two-year-old male crossbills are predominantly greenish yellow or orange. The flight call is a typical metallic 'chip'. The greenfinch-like song is irregular and hasty, including twitterings, piercing notes and occasional calls. A typical denizen of coniferous forests, depending on cone seeds, mainly from spruce trees. Occasionally crossbill species go on invasion-like wanderings (irruptions) due usually to a shortage of food in autumn. Many reach eastern Britain and remain to breed.

Parrot crossbill *Loxia pytyopsittacus*

18 cm

Very similar to the crossbill – considered by some to be the species breeding in highland Scotland – but older birds have a thicker bill. The note is deeper, but its variations in both species often make it impossible to distinguish between them. Prefers pine woods.

Distribution maps on p. 116

Crossbill   juvenile

♂

♀

♂

Rosefinch (scarlet grosbeak)

Crossbill ♂

Parrot crossbill

♂

Crossbill

♀

Siskin

Greenfinch

Serin

Goldfinch

Redpoll

Linnet

Chaffinch ♂

Brambling ♂ winter

Bullfinch ♂

Hawfinch

♀

♂

Rosefinch/scarlet grosbeak ♂

Crossbill

Ornithological & Conservation Societies in Britain and Ireland

Most countries and some major towns and cities have their own ornithological society: your library should be able to provide the address. Usually these societies hold regular indoor and field meetings – an ideal introduction to the area and the subject – and publish regular reports.

National bodies:

British Trust for Ornithology, Beech Grove, Tring, Herts.
(organize bird ringing, censuses and a wide variety of studies designed for cooperative participation by amateurs. *Bird Study* quarterly, *BTO News* every two months).

Irish Wildbird Conservancy, Royal Irish Academy, 19 Dawson Street, Dublin 2.
(fulfils a similar role in Ireland to the B.T.O.).

Royal Society for the Protection of Birds, The Lodge, Sandy, Beds.
(reserve network available to members, junior branch Young Ornithologists' Club organizes cooperative fieldwork. Colour magazine *Birds* quarterly).

Wildfowl Trust, Slimbridge, Gloucestershire.
(network of wildfowl reserves and collections available, organize winter wildfowl counts. Regular bulletin, *Wildfowl News*, and *Wildfowl*, published annually).

Further Reading

The following selection of books is suggested for you to follow up your interest in birds and their lives. Some deal with identification, some with fieldwork and equipment, and some with biology and ecology. All will prove useful sources of further titles.

Barnes, J. A. G., *The Titmice of the British Isles*, David & Charles, 1975.

Batten, L., Flegg, J., Sorensen, J., Wareing, M., Watson, D. and Wright, D., *Birdwatchers' Year*, T. & A. D. Poyser, 1973.

Brown, L., *The British Birds of Prey*, Collins, 1976.

Bruun, B. and Singer, A., *The Hamlyn Guide to the Birds of Britain and Europe*, Hamlyn, 1974.

Campbell, B., and Ferguson-Lees, J., *A Field Guide to Birds' Nests*, Constable, 1972.

Fisher, J. and Flegg, J., *Watching birds*, T. & A. D. Poyser, 1974; Penguin Books, 1978 (in paperback).

Flegg, J., *Discovering Bird Watching*, Shire Publications, 1973.

Flegg, J. J. M., *Binoculars, Cameras and Telescopes*, B.T.O. Field Guide, 1971.

Flegg, J. J. M. and Glue, D. E., *Nestboxes*, B.T.O. Field Guide, 1971.

Fry, C. H. and Flegg, J. J. M., *World Atlas of Birds*, Mitchell Beazley, 1974.

Gooders, J., *Where to Watch Birds*, Deutsch, 1967; Pan Books, 1977 (in paperback).

Gooders, J., *Where to Watch Birds in Europe*, Deutsch, 1970; Pan Books, 1977 (in paperback).

Heinzel, H., Fitter, R. and Parslow, J., *The Birds of Britain and Europe*, Collins, 1972.

Hollom, P. A. D., *The Popular Handbook of British Birds*, H. F. & G. Witherby, 1971.

Hollom, P. A. D., *The Popular Handbook of Rarer British Birds*, H. F. & G. Witherby, 1970.

Lack, D., *Population Studies of Birds*, Oxford University Press, 1966.

Moreau, R. E., *The Paleartic-African Bird Migration System*, Academic

Newton, I., *Finches*, Collins, 1973.

Sharrock, J. T. R. (ed.), *The Atlas of Breeding Birds in Britain and Ireland*, B.T.O., 1977.

Simms, E., *Woodland Birds*, Collins, 1971.

Thomson, A. L., *A New Dictionary of Birds*, Nelson, 1964.

Voous, K. H., *Atlas of European Birds*, Nelson, 1960.

Welty, J. C., *The Life of Birds*, Saunders, 1975.

Witherby, H. F., Jourdain, F. C. R., Ticehurst, N. F. and Tucker, B. W., *The Handbook of British Birds*, 5 vols, H. F. & G. Witherby, 1938–41.

Index